GOD'S CONDITIONS FOR PROSPERITY

What Is Real Prosperity?

Charles Hunter

Published by Hunter Books
City of Light
201 McClellan Road
Kingwood, Texas 77339, U.S.A.

BOOKS
BY CHARLES♥FRANCES HUNTER

A CONFESSION A DAY KEEPS THE DEVIL AWAY
ANGELS ON ASSIGNMENT
ARE YOU TIRED?
BORN AGAIN! WHAT DO YOU MEAN?
COME ALIVE
DON'T LIMIT GOD
FOLLOW ME
GOD IS FABULOUS
GOD'S ANSWER TO FAT...LOOSE IT!
GOD'S CONDITIONS FOR PROSPERITY
HOT LINE TO HEAVEN
HOW TO MAKE YOUR MARRIAGE EXCITING
IF YOU REALLY LOVE ME...
IMPOSSIBLE MIRACLES
IN JESUS' NAME!
IT'S SO SIMPLE (formerly HANG LOOSE WITH JESUS)
LET'S GO WITNESSING (formerly GO, MAN, GO)
MEMORIZING MADE EASY
MY LOVE AFFAIR WITH CHARLES
NUGGETS OF TRUTH
POSSESSING THE MIND OF CHRIST
P.T.L.A. (Praise the Lord, Anyway!)
SIMPLE AS A.B.C.
SINCE JESUS PASSED BY
the fabulous SKINNIE MINNIE RECIPE BOOK
SUPERNATURAL HORIZONS (from Glory to Glory)
THE DEVIL WANTS YOUR MIND
THE TWO SIDES OF A COIN
THIS WAY UP!
TO HEAL THE SICK
WHY SHOULD "I" SPEAK IN TONGUES???

In the event your Christian Bookstore does not have any of the books written by Charles and Frances Hunter or published by Hunter Books, please write for price list and order form from HUNTER BOOKS. For information about Charles' and Frances' video teaching tapes, audio tapes, and price list of Hunter Books, write to: HUNTER BOOKS, 201 McClellan Road, Kingwood, Texas 77339, U.S.A

ISBN 0-917726-41-3

Contents

Chapter One

What Is
Real Prosperity?

Do you really want to be prosperous? Then ask yourself, "What *is* real prosperity?"

When we say prosperity, what do we really mean? The first thing we think of is living on Nob Hill in a big mansion, and driving forty-nine Cadillacs plus two Rolls Royces.

One time when I was operating as a certified public accountant, I was working for a multi-ultra-multi-millionaire. He had lots of money, more than he could ever spend even the interest on. He was super rich. He said to me, "Charles, don't ever lose your desire to work, because the most miserable thing you can ever do is to lose that desire!"

That is tremendous advice. Some people

think that the ultimate in prosperity is when you can retire and quit work. But literally, that is the farthest thing from the truth. It is a lie of the devil. The Ten Commandments tell us, *"Six days you shall labor and do all your work, but the seventh day is a sabbath of the Lord your God; in it you shall not do any work...."* (Exodus 20:9, 10 NASB).

The problem is that we stopped working on the sixth day, then we reduced it to five or four, and we got into a lot of problems and misery because we didn't work on the sixth day. We thought rest would come on the seventh day, but if you loaf on the sixth, you get miserable on the seventh. You get bored, and that isn't prosperity.

Prosperity has many facets; it is expensive, but is easily available to us. Too often, however, we have false notions about things we think are necessary in order to have prosperity; we are utter failures, no matter how rich in substance we might find ourselves to be.

The dictionary says that prosperity is a state of being prosperous; advance or gain in anything good or desirable; successful progress in any business or enterprise. Prosperity means success.

Prosperity means abundance. But what does abundance mean? Great plenty, an overflowing quantity, ample sufficiency, abundance of heart, more than enough.

God can do all things. He can do miracles. He can do anything. God is the only one who can give true abundance.

Jesus said, *"The thief cometh not, but for to steal, and to kill, and to destroy; I am come that they might have life, and that they might have it more abundantly"* (John 10:10 KJV).

That is real prosperity. That is real success. But what are the conditions for receiving abundant life? Do you just suddenly wake up some morning and say, "I'm abundantly rich?" Suppose you were dealing with finances and someone died and the lawyer came to you and said, "Here is the substance of his will. You are now a millionaire!" Is that the way to have abundance? Well, that would be abundance in one area of your life, wouldn't it?

We heard a testimony recently about a man who had worked very hard for two or three years in a new company. He was a scientist who was working on many different projects when he suddenly broke through with an outstanding invention. He went to bed one night with just enough money to live on, and the next morning he was a millionaire.

Someone asked him on television, "How does it feel to be prosperous? Do you feel different now that you are a millionaire?"

He said:

No, really it doesn't make a bit of difference to me. I was having the needs that I had met. I was eating regularly. I was sleepng regularly. I was clothed well. I was housed well, and I was happy in my work. It didn't change that. It's nice to have security, but it won't affect my life at all! I'm going right on working to develop other new inventions which will bless someone else.

He had a giving heart. One of God's great and mighty conditions is that you must have the ability to give in order to receive. Jesus said, "It is better to give than to receive."

Jesus showed us many other conditions which give us prosperity. I suppose one of the greatest times of prosperity I have ever had was when everything seemed to go wrong. Problems hit. Finances were low. My health was giving me a problem. I was working hard. The pieces were not fitting together. We were struggling with personnel. We were struggling with everything there was, but when I suddenly looked up and saw God, I had peace. I wasn't worried about the outcome. I wasn't worried about what was going to happen. I wasn't worried about how I was going to meet the next payroll for the company, although it had to be met. There was no way I could avoid meeting it, and yet because I had peace, I had prosperity — real prosperity.

When I was a child, I had a dread of being drafted into the military and sent into the war where I would have to go out and shoot people. I had nightmares a time or two, thinking I was out on the front line shooting people, and I didn't want to shoot people. That wasn't abundance at all, but when I did enter the Air Force, I didn't have any fear, because I was trusting in God. That is real abundance. That's the ultimate in prosperity.

Chapter Two

Prosperity: Lost and Found

Genuine prosperity lies in trusting and obeying God as our supplier, the one who provides all of our needs, according to his riches in glory by Christ Jesus. That is real prosperity.

The first prosperity recorded in the word of God is right in the beginning. There were two young kids in the Garden of Eden, and who could have ever wanted anything more? A young married couple, Adam and Eve. They didn't have to worry about building a home. They didn't have to worry about whether they had furniture. They didn't have to worry about jobs. They didn't have to worry about clothes. They just walked about in the Garden of Eden and enjoyed it! They walked in the cool of the evening with God and had the world's most delicious fruit to eat. They had *everything*. They were prosperous. In all of the history of all the earth, they were without a doubt the richest people on earth. And yet they didn't have even a two-dollar bill in their pocket. (They didn't even have pockets.) They had everything because God provided them with everything they needed.

If they had just obeyed God, we could have had the same Garden of Eden, expanded to where 4.4 billion people could have still been living in that prosperity. But they broke their relationship to prosperity. They sinned. They rebelled against almighty God, and when you rebel against God, you lose all the benefits of God. If you obey God, you become his child and all of his inheritance becomes yours. Everything that God has is ours when we are obedient to him, but when we rebel and put another god before him, then we are removed from the blessings of the family of God.

We are removed from his protection, and abundance becomes actual poverty. We are poor. Adam and Eve, who were millionaires —billionaires—with everything they needed, suddenly found themselves without anything. In that one moment of sin, all the prosperity God had provided for mankind was lost.

Back in 1929 and 1930, many people

jumped off skyscrapers when the stockmarket crashed, because people who had been multi-millionaires were suddenly left with nothing. Their pride was hurt, and the thing they had thought was their prosperity was gone, and they discovered they had nothing left. They were living in poverty. They had nothing, nothing, nothing, left! And the reason they didn't have anything left is that they based their prosperity on the wrong thing, the wrong person, the wrong condition.

Well, then, how can we be prosperous? How can we walk into this kingdom of prosperity, this living in abundance in everything that we do? How can we do that when Adam and Eve destroyed all of that prosperity? The whole world banking system failed when Adam and Eve sinned. God said, "Here's a whole orchard of fruit. You can have anything you want, except the fruit from this one tree."

They had everything they needed, but because of greed, they disobeyed God and ate of the forbidden fruit, and poverty struck instead of abundance.

Let's review a little story about Abraham. He was one of the most successful people of all times. He had an abundance of everything. He had a happy family. Even when he was an old man, he and his wife produced a child. He had the whole world at his fingertips, and God blessed him abundantly. What was the condition, the source of his prosperity?

Abraham is the father of faith. He trusted God. He believed that there *was* a God—that there was *one* God—that he could *communicate* with that God—that he could *live* for that God—that he could *obey* that God—that he could *hear* that God speak.

God began to deal with Abraham, and Abraham had to meet certain conditions. One of the hardest decisions that was ever placed before Abraham was when God called on him to lay his son of the promise on the altar. God had promised that he would give him a son who was to be his heritage. God had said that through him would come so many children that they would be more plentiful than the grains of sand out on the beach, and yet God spoke to him and said, "Go kill your only son!"

Is that abundance? If you had to kill one member of your family, would that be the abundant life? No, but the *faith* that Abraham had was abundant life. The most precious thing he had was his only son. The action that he had to take would have brought poverty into his heart. If his son was taken away from him, he would have lost everything that made him happy, but he was willing to give *all* in order to do what God wanted him to do. He was willing to trust God as his source of everything, and by faith he believed that if he plunged the knife into the heart of his son and killed him, God would raise him from the dead. God let him meet a test. When he met that test, the condition for prosperity, then God opened up a new abundance of prosperity.

Obedience was the thing that caused Abraham to maintain his abundant life, his riches, his prosperity. But what would have happened if at that crucial moment he had said, "God, I can't do it!" He would have lost his prosperity—his abundant life.

When Abraham was old and ready to depart from this earth as a human being, he wanted to do something for his son Isaac. Abraham wanted him to have a wife; but he had been instructed by the almighty God that Isaac was not to marry a foreigner from the Canaan land, so he instructed his trustworthy servant to go and find a suitable wife for his son.

The servant's first response was, "But what if I can't find the wife that God wants him to have?" Be very careful whenever you hear the words, "But what if?" As long as you operate in the "but what if's" and you're in doubt, you cannot have the abundant life. The servant was disturbed. What would happen to him? Well, if a servant didn't obey his master, he could be killed. He knew he had to obey.

Let's look at this *prosperity story* in The Living Bible starting with the first verse of the twenty-fourth chapter of Genesis.

> *Abraham was now a very old man, and God blessed him in every way.* [God had given him *prosperity* in every way. Why? What were his conditions for prosperity?] *One day Abraham said to his household administrator, who was his oldest servant, "Swear by Jehovah, the God of heaven and earth, that you will not let my son marry one of those local girls, these Canaanites. Go instead to my homeland, to my relatives, and find a wife for him there."*

> *"But suppose I can't find a girl who will come so far from home?" the servant asked. "Then shall I take Isaac there, to live among your relatives?"*

> *"No!" Abraham warned. "Be careful that you don't do that under any circumstance."*

Abraham had a reason for being so specific and here it is:

"For the Lord God of heaven told me to leave that land and my people, and promised to give me and my children this land."

Abraham knew what God had promised; he knew what prosperity was and how to attain it. He knew God's conditions for prosperity. He knew God said to obey his laws.

Through telescopic spiritual eyes God was giving him a view of what Jesus would do to bring ultimate prosperity to all of us. Jesus was to give us life, and life abundantly, if we would serve him with complete obedience.

Abraham also knew that if he didn't do what God said, he would lose everything. Later the children of Israel found this out when, after being in slavery in Egypt so long, God led them out. Because they disobeyed him, they never found the prosperity of the land of milk and honey that they could have had. They failed to trust God. They lost their opportunity for prosperity because they failed to believe God as Abraham had done before them. They did not meet the conditions for prosperity.

Continuing with Genesis 24, Abraham said:

"He will send his angel on ahead of you,

*and he will see to it that you find a girl
from there to be my son's wife. But if you
don't succeed, then you are free from this
oath; but under no circumstances are you
to take my son there."*

*So the servant vowed to follow
Abraham's instructions.*

Notice that the servant knew the conditions for
his prosperity, too.

*He took with him ten of Abraham's cam-
els loaded with samples of the best of everything his master owned, and journeyed
to Iraq, to Nahor's village. There he made
the camels kneel down outside the town,
beside a spring. It was evening, and the
women of the village were coming to draw
water.*

*"O Jehovah, the God of my master," he
prayed, "show kindness to my master
Abraham and help me to accomplish the
purpose of my journey."*

This servant knew the source of prosperity.

*"See, here I am, standing beside this
spring, and the girls of the village are*

coming out to draw water. This is my request: When I ask one of them for a drink and she says, 'Yes, certainly, and I will water your camels too!'—let her be the one you have appointed as Isaac's wife. That is how I will know."

As he was still speaking to the Lord about this, a beautiful young girl named Rebekah arrived with a water jug on her shoulder and filled it at the spring. [Her father was Bethuel the son of Nahor and his wife Milcah.] Running over to her, the servant asked her for a drink.

"Certainly, sir," she said, and quickly lowered the jug for him to drink. Then she said, "I'll draw water for your camels, too, until they have enough!"

Glory to God! Talk about prosperity. This servant found what he was looking for, and Rebekah, who was willing to give even more than this stranger asked for, was about to be blessed as well!

So she emptied the jug into the watering trough and ran down to the spring again and kept carrying water to the camels until they had enough. The servant said no more, but watched her carefully to see if she would finish the job, so that he would know whether she was the one. Then at last, when the camels had finished drinking, he produced a quarter-ounce gold earring and two five-ounce golden bracelets for her wrists.

This servant wanted to please his master, and God provided prosperity for him. If we really want to please our Master, then we, too, can ask God for anything within his plan and he will gladly, abundantly give it to us like he did to Abraham's servant. Oh, God, we love you for your loving care for those who meet your conditions to receive that mighty love. Thank you, Father, for your overwhelming prosperity when we meet your simple conditions.

"Whose daughter are you, miss?" he asked. "Would your father have any room to put us up for the night?"

"My father is Bethuel, the son of Milcah, the wife of Nahor," she replied. "Yes, we have plenty of straw and food for the camels, and a guest room."

The man stood there a moment with head bowed, worshipping Jehovah. "Thank

you, Lord God of my master Abraham,"
he prayed; "thank you for being so kind
and true to him, and for leading me
straight to the family of my master's rela-
tives."

Oh, the simplicity of God's conditions for
prosperity. This servant knew that he wanted
to please his master, and look what God did
for him. The servant also was quick to ac-
knowledge the source of prosperity he had
found—for his master, but also for himself.
His master's son was to get the beautiful wife
God selected for him, but the servant received
a mighty gift also. His prosperity was not only
that he was successful in his mission for his
master, but he was blessed by God with that
inner prosperity of the satisfaction, peace,
thrill, love, joy that is so great that only our
God can give it to a human. If you have known
that intimate personal love God floods you
with when you have pleased him, you know
that there is no prosperity on earth so great
and so blessed.

In the 35th verse the servant said:

And Jehovah has overwhelmed my master
with blessings so that he is a great man
among the people of his land. God has

given him flocks of sheep and herds of cattle, and a fortune in silver and gold, and many slaves and camels and donkeys.

There are few people on earth today, if any, that have the prosperity of Abraham. How did he acquire such wealth? By obedience to his God. The conditions for our prosperity today are the same as Abraham met; willing and total obedience to Jehovah, the living mighty God whom we serve. That kind of prosperity cannot be measured. It cannot be contained in a bank or in houses and land. It cannot be depleted; it keeps getting more blessed as we give more of our love to our Master.

Frances and I were in the elite executive offices of a professional person recently. Everything in the office was new, the finest, and the latest model. This person had just moved into the penthouse of a skyscraper building overlooking the giant multiplex of Houston's richest downtown area. We remarked that the offices were superbly beautiful when the owner said, "I have everything I need and what I don't have I don't want."

Our hearts cried because really the only thing needed was Jesus, and he was the only thing the person did not have.

It is through Isaac and Rebekah that we have our inheritance of a continuing life that

God promised Abraham. But it is through Abraham's obedience and faith in the God in whom he so totally believed that we have our inheritance in Jesus. This prosperity lasts forever and ever and is beyond measure. There is really no abundance, no prosperity any place or any way except that given by God through Jesus.

Look at the provisions for that kind of prosperity. Abraham and his faithful servant heard God, they trusted God, they believed God, they obeyed God even unto death if necessary, because they wanted to. They found out what God wanted and their only desire was to please him, not themselves. Do you realize that we can ask God for great earthly prosperity and limit him thereby? If you open your imaginations and dream up the greatest prosperity you can think of and if God gave you that, you would limit the desires of God.

Chapter 3

Discovery
of Gold

His unlimited prosperity is promised us, with a
condition, in Malachi 3:10 TLB:

> *Bring all the tithes into the storehouse so
> that there will be food enough in my Tem-
> ple;* [God's condition] *if you do, I will
> open up the windows of heaven for you
> and pour out a blessing so great you won't
> have room enough to take it in! Try it!
> Let me prove it to you!*

When I read that promise in Malachi, I
thought, " 'Bring in your whole tithe'—that
means give all your life, everything to God."
That's what I wanted to do more than any-

thing else. Somehow I was impressed that I should give all of myself; I didn't really notice nor desire that God should give me blessings more than I could imagine. I already had a beautiful home, three cars when I only needed one, a prospering CPA business where my clients loved me and I loved the work. I had good health; I was happy; and I had a host of friends. I had found a new personal relationship with God and Jesus. I was abundantly blessed. I had everything I wanted or needed and I really wasn't looking for more than I already had.

I was determined that I would meditate day and night in God's word because God had spoken to me and told me to go into his word and listen to no man and he would tell me what *he* wanted me to know. That was all that mattered to me, and I read night and day. I couldn't get enough of the Bible.

If you looked at my circumstances during that time, you wouldn't call it abundance. My wife fell sick and died of cancer. Was that abundance? The prosperity I had during what the world might describe as the opposite, was that God had said, "Charles, let me do this my way" and I was pleased to let him do anything he wanted to his way. Why should I question him? Abraham didn't. His servant didn't. Jesus didn't.

The promises God gave to Abraham are also still for us today.

That the blessing of Abraham might come on the Gentiles through Jesus Christ, that we might receive the promise of the Spirit through faith (Galatians 3:14 KJV).

Because God and Jesus want to overwhelm us with their greatest blessings, I can just imagine them sitting on their throne, chatting about things on earth and noticing me. I can hear them saying, "Charles really means it when he says he wants to please us. He is pouring himself into the Bible to search for our desires. His heart is right, so let's find him a special gift."

I can see them in my imagination going into the storehouse of their heavenly treasury and looking around for this special gift. Jesus probably said, "Do you think this mansion alongside a mountain brook would make him more happy? No, he has a beautiful home on Memorial Drive that he loves, and he has told us he has no desire for anything more than he already has. We have already given him a fine prospering business, his home amid the trees he loves, good health, happiness. He keeps telling us he just wants to find ways to make us happy. That mansion wouldn't make any difference to him.

"How about giving him a new Rolls Royce? No, he has three cars and he doesn't even need but one, and he doesn't care about showing off his possessions.

"We could make his stock value go up and the value of his house and land go up and make him rich! But he doesn't even care about that anymore. He has already told us that he would give it away if we wanted him to. All he wants to do is look for ways to please us."

Then both of them must have jumped up and shouted at the same time. "There it is! There it is! There it is!" They both rushed over to the big window of heaven. Jesus got hold of one side and God the other and they slid it open as wide as they could and shoved Frances right into my arms! Glory to God, that's prosperity at its peak! Who could ask for anything more?

Abundant prosperity? Frances is a blessing far beyond anything I could ever imagine or dream. That gift is something like Jesus saying, if you obey the first two commandments, all the others will follow. When they blessed me with Frances, I found the nature of Jesus in her, all that could ever be described as prosperity. I found love, joy, peace, patience, kindness, goodness, faithfulness, gentleness, self-control, all these and anything else God could think of.

Why did they choose to give me such a blessing? Because I had obeyed them in every way I knew, from my heart, and I trusted them to take all of my life and do with it what they wanted to without consideration of what they would do for me. That's a condition for prosperity. Also, I get more joy out of doing things to make Frances happy than anything she could do for me. That is a principle of God: Giving will always bring returns. If you give, you will receive, but God wants us to give without thought of what he can do in return. We limit him if we look first for what he will do for us if we will do something for him. He can outgive us a hundred to one or even more. Our attitude is a condition of prosperity.

Chapter Four

Understanding Successful People

I have always been told that if I wanted success, I should look at the person who has attained success and see why it worked for him. Because of this, I began to look at the successful characters in the Bible because there must be a reason they found the prosperity they did.

Let's look at Joseph. He was successful. He prospered mightily. What caused him to have so much in his favor? What conditions for prosperity did he observe and do? This story is found in Genesis, chapters 37 to 50.

Joseph was loved by his father more than the other children of Jacob because he was born in his old age. This kind of special love is prosperity. Joseph would report to his father some of the things his brothers would do wrong, and it caused his brothers to dislike him. This grew into hate and jealousy until they even wanted to kill him. Would you say Joseph had prosperity at that time? Did he have abundance? He must have lived in fear of the danger from them. They were probably mean to him every day. *Do* you think Joseph thought, "I am living prosperously!"

Sure enough, one day they decided to kill him, but one brother said, "No, let's do something else. Let's throw him into the well over there and then dip his coat into the blood of an animal and send it home to our father with the message that an animal killed him." Can you imagine how successful Joseph felt at that time?

But Joseph trusted God. He didn't know God's plan, but he trusted him with his very life. His father had taught him well to believe in God. Although Joseph didn't realize it, God caused merchants to come by and purchase him as a slave.

As a slave, Joseph worked hard for his master. That is a condition of the Bible for prosperity. God's laws and nature were implanted into the heart of Joseph. Later, God put this law in Ephesians 6:5 *"Slaves, obey your masters; be eager to give them your very best. Serve them as you would Christ"* (TLB).

Because he obeyed God's laws, because he obeyed his master and worked hard, he was promoted to the head position in Potiphar's house. Potiphar was a member of the personal staff of Pharaoh, the king of Egypt. He was the captain of the king's bodyguard and his chief executioner.

> *The Lord greatly blessed Joseph there in the home of his master, so that everything he did succeeded. Potiphar noticed this and realized that the Lord was with Joseph in a very special way. So Joseph naturally became quite a favorite with him. Soon he was put in charge of the administration of Potiphar's household, and all of his business affairs. At once the Lord began blessing Potiphar for Joseph's sake. All his household affairs began to run smoothly, his crops flourished and his flocks multiplied* (Genesis 39:2-5 TLB).

This really was abundant prosperity, wasn't it? Potiphar trusted Joseph. But Joseph was a very handsome young man and Potiphar's wife was a beautiful woman without too many scruples. One day they were alone in the big house.

> *[She] began making eyes at Joseph and suggested that he come and sleep with her. Joseph refused. "Look," he told her, "my master trusts me with everything in the entire household; he himself has no more authority here than I have! He has held back nothing from me except you yourself because you are his wife. How can I do such a wicked thing as this? It would be a great sin against God."* (Genesis 39:7-9 TLB).

In spite of his resistance and keeping away from her as much as he could, she finally demanded, "Sleep with me." When he tried to flee, she grabbed his jacket and held it. When he ran away, she began screaming and when others came to her, she said, *"He tried to rape me, but when I screamed, he ran, and forgot to take his jacket"* (verse 15).

Prosperity was working for him at that time?

What were his conditions for prosperity? Under the circumstances it looked like he had *had* it. Back into prison and chains he went. Who would ever believe God was still on his side? Does God's promise of prosperity work at a time like this? Joseph was obedient, fair, just, faithful, loyal, and honest with God and man. But apparently it was not working for him. Did you ever think about God's prosperity in your life? I did, but at that time, and every time I have been tempted to think that, I simply said, "God, I will be faithful to you no matter what happens." God always comes through with blessings when I continue to trust him.

Joseph got prosperous again, because God gave him favor in prison with the chief jailer. In fact, the entire prison administration was soon turned over to him. The Lord was with him so that everything ran smoothly and well. Sure, God's prosperity works if we continue to meet his conditions of trusting and obeying his laws, his nature and his principles.

How would you like it if you had a chance to get out of prison, but some guy forgot for two years to tell the right people to free you? That's what happened, and can you imagine being in jail for two years and calling that prosperity?

But Pharaoh had a dream and he needed a dream interpreter. Because Joseph received the interpretation from God, again God's prosperity came to Joseph, and he was not only freed from jail, but was elevated to the highest ranking person in the land under the king. It was through this that Joseph was able to follow God's instructions so that all of Egypt was saved from famine through his wisdom, and eventually Joseph's family was united and saved from starvation.

You have seen an overview of the entire life of one of God's most successful people, and yet he was in and out of prison or slavery a great portion of his life. So what prosperity did he attain in life, and what were the conditions under which he attained his abundance?

Listen to the greatness of the nature of God in Joseph as he revealed his identity to the brothers who sold him into slavery:

> *"I am Joseph, your brother whom you sold into Egypt! But don't be angry with yourselves that you did this to me, for God did it! He sent me here ahead of you to preserve your lives. These two years of famine will grow to seven, during which there will be neither plowing nor harvest. God has sent me here to keep you and your families alive, so that you will become a great nation. Yes, it was God who sent me here, not you!"* (Genesis 45:4-7 TLB).

God looks over the entire lifetime of each of us, and he knows what is necessary to carry out his eternal plan of redemption for his people. Greater it is to serve his purposes than to have a continuous lifetime of wealth and ease. Never in his lifetime did Joseph fail to follow the will of God, even though many times and for long times he never saw earthly evidence of prosperity. Yet, in his own heart he must always have had peace in knowing he was in the perfect will of his Father.

Many times when Frances and I have problems of finance, health, business operations in our ministry, or other negative attacks on our lives, when we take it to God, he gives a great peace, a calm in our spirits. That is our personal signal that the answer is on the way. Further, even if that peace does not come as soon as we think it should, we have God's word, which gives us the assurance that he will take care of all our needs according to his riches in glory by Christ Jesus.

If someone placed an unlimited amount of funds on deposit in a bank, and the bank informed you that you could write as many checks as you desired for any amount you wanted or needed, would you say you have abundant prosperity? Who could do better than that? God can!

Joseph obeyed God and followed the principles of giving and giving and giving, and he continually served others whether he was in prison or heading the government. His circumstances made no difference in his desire to please God and obey him.

Because Joseph believed God and obeyed him, God always took care of his needs. He could have had wealth and earthly fulfillment by his opportunities to get rich; he could have stolen grain, he could have slept with a beautiful woman in satisfaction of lust of the flesh, he had the wealth of a nation at his fingertips and could have become a millionaire. All this and more could have been Joseph's, but God had an eternal plan to fulfill and a people who needed him. He chose a man whom he could trust. God was pleased, and when God is pleased he will truly open the windows of heaven and pour out blessings more than we can ever dream or imagine. The condition God set for Joseph was that of trust. Joseph met that condition, and God fulfilled his promise of prosperity for him.

God's plans are preordained. He will carry out every single detail of his plan for mankind, his fellowship with his creation, his redemption of mankind. He does not predestine or preordain a human being, but he selects certain people and if they do not do his job, he will pass them by and find someone who will obey him to the very end.

When we find God's best, we will find it in being trustworthy in his service; then he will choose us to become a part of his plan to build historic steps into eternity. That's eternal prosperity.

I plan to meet all of God's conditions for prosperity. Do you?

Chapter Five

Choosing Blessings or Curses

Perhaps the clearest and most simple of all places in the Bible to find God's conditions for prosperity is in the book of Deuteronomy, chapter 28. The first fourteen verses tell us how to become prosperous. Verses fifteen to the end of the chapter tell us of the abject poverty we will have if we do not follow the conditions of prosperity in the first fourteen verses. It is that simple.

> *If you fully obey all of these commandments of the Lord your God, the laws I am declaring to you today, God will transform you into the greatest nation in the world. These are the blessings that will*

come upon you: (Deuteronomy 28:1, 2
TLB).

Then he goes on to tell about every kind of
blessing you can imagine. In verse nine he
says, *"He will change you into a holy people
dedicated to himself; this he has promised to
do if you will only obey him and walk in his
ways."*

Do you see how simple he makes it? Just
obey what he has set forth for us, and do you
believe God only wants what is good for us?
Isn't it foolish to even consider doing something against God's law just to get punished
when we can have him on our side helping us
into prosperity?

And how much more prosperous can we
get than to be changed into a holy people
dedicated to God? Did you notice the simple
conditions he made in exchange for him making us holy? *"...if you will only obey him and
walk in his ways."* God is so plain in his word,
and is so simple in his requirements.

Look what else he lists under his prosperity offer:

> *The Lord will give you an abun-
> dance of good things in the land,
> just as he promised: many children,*

*many cattle, and abundant crops. He will
open to you his wonderful treasury of rain
in the heavens, to give you fine crops every season. He will bless everything you
do*—and what are his only conditions for
you to walk in this abundant prosperity?
Just simple obedience! *"But each of these
blessings depends on your not turning
aside in any way from the laws I have giv-
en you; and you must never worship other
gods,"* (Deuteronomy 28:11, 14 TLB).

What are God's laws? You can sum them up,
Jesus said, in two laws:

*"Love the Lord your God with all your
heart, soul, and mind." This is the first
and greatest commandment. The second
most important is similar: "Love your
neighbor as much as you love yourself."
All the other commandments and all the
demands of the prophets stem from these
two laws and are fulfilled if you obey
them. Keep only these and you will find
that you are obeying all the others* (Matthew 22:37-40 TLB).

When you think of the conditions of prosperity, of obeying the commandments or laws of

God, think with me a moment about what Jesus meant by obeying these two laws. If you truly love your father, mother, sister, brother, wife, husband, children or someone else, don't you want to do everything you can to please them? I have found that because I want to do everything I can to make Frances happy, the more I do for her, the more she wants to do for me. I do it because I want to—not to get love or attention in return, but that law of giving love still works.

That's why it works when you love the Lord your God with all your heart, soul, and mind.

If I paid more attention to some other woman than I did Frances, do you think I would prosper in receiving her best love? No way. Do you see why it is important to God that we put no other gods before him? He wants all of us and all our love, but in exchange for that simple little thing, he promises all the blessings and more that he lists in the first fourteen verses of Deuteronomy 28. Why not try that route into abundant prosperity? The conditions are easy and even doing those conditions brings prosperity. You just can't lose by blessing God. His exchange rate is too good to miss.

But just in case you want to be so foolish as to not choose the first fourteen verses of blessings, take a look at the consequences, at the road to poverty and misery.

*If you won't listen to the Lord your God
and won't obey these laws I am giving you
today, then all of these curses shall come
upon you* (Deuteronomy 28:15 TLB).

Who wants God to place a curse upon us? God
has no desire to do this, but when he made
laws he made them perfect to perform abundantly for us, not against us. Gravity is a law
of God. Once he set this law into motion, it
will not be changed until God wants to change
it. Our obedience or disobedience will not
change that law. God's attitude toward us
whether we obey or disobey will not change
that law. The law is good and perfect. But,
when we go against that law it will do us harm.
Notice that God doesn't harm us. We harm
ourselves by disobedience.

God's law that we should love our neighbor as we love ourselves is a perfect law. God
set the law into motion, and it will always
work for our good if we do it. If we do harm to
our neighbor, the law will work against us.
That isn't God's fault. He designed the law to
work wonders for us and to give us the greatest
prosperity in our neighborhood. Try putting
that law to work for you, and you will see how
your neighbors respond.

If you want prosperity to come your way,
just do what Jesus said in those two command-

ments, and watch God command blessings to come your way.

Often people hear a good prosperity teacher say you can claim your blessings from God. Just give your money to God, and he will give it back so abundantly that you can live in financial riches. Well, there's nothing wrong with that statement, and there's nothing wrong with that law. But don't forget God's conditions that make the law work for you.

Your car will work for you if it is in good running order and is supplied with gasoline or other fuel. But you have to do more than just get into it and say, "Car, take me to my desired destination." Sure it will work, but not without you meeting its conditions. You have to set the force, the power that makes the car go, into motion by igniting the fuel that turns the shaft that moves the wheels. You have to work with the laws that make the automobile function. If you sit there and say, "Car, in the name of Jesus, I command you to take me to the store" it won't work for you.

Why won't it work for you? Is it because you have a lack of faith? Is it because God just doesn't love you any more? Is it because of your saying something bad to your spouse on the way out the door? No, that car could care less about those things. All it needs you to do is obey its laws.

God says:

*My people are destroyed for lack of
knowledge; because you (the priestly nation) have rejected knowledge, I will also
reject you, that you shall be no priest to
Me; seeing you have forgotten the law of
your God, I will also forget your children.
The more they increased and multiplied
(in prosperity and power), the more they
sinned against Me; I will change their
glory into shame* (Hosea 4:6, 7 Amp.).

Notice in those Scriptures that it was the fault
of the people that God could not bless them
"in prosperity and power." God cannot operate against his laws. He honors his word,
praise his holy name. We can always depend
on God—can God always depend on us?

If you didn't know how to start the motor
on your car, you would lack knowledge that
would keep you from enjoying the prosperity
of driving the car. A condition for using your
car is that you know how to use it. A condition
of getting God's word to work for you is
knowing how to make it work. You need to
study the instructions or listen carefully to an
instructor to drive a car or to set into motion
the laws of God's promises.

If you want to be able to attain riches by

claiming God's promises of a hundredfold return, read the instructions very careful-ly—all of them. Meditate day and night in his instruction book, his word, and you will dis-cover some of the laws and conditions of the laws working in your life. Riches come by obe-dience to all of God's laws combined, not by one or two verses. Then you also need to un-derstand what riches are and which ones you need. Riches in money, homes, cars, and other earthly possessions are not bad in themselves. In fact, they are good, but they may not be what you need most.

We have had people come to us for heal-ing when they were almost dead from some disease. They would gladly part with all their riches to get their health and life back.

The greatest riches you can have are not riches in things, but in blessings from God. Now, don't get the idea I think God wants you to be living in poverty. I believe God wants us to prosper in our earthly living. But some of us would put earthly riches above those things which God knows are best for us. Too often, the more we increase and multiply in prosperi-ty and power, the more we sin against God, as God said in Hosea 4:7.

God's laws provide for a balanced life. If the plant life in a fish aquarium is out of bal-ance, the fish will die. If we don't listen to all of God's word so we will understand his balance, we can die from lack of knowledge about how to live in his balanced life here on earth. That's why God says,

> *Beloved, I wish above all things that thou mayest prosper and be in health, even as thy soul prospereth* (III John 2 KJV).

God can bless some people with greater earthly possessions because they are balanced in their understanding of the total Bible principles and because they can love God more than the god of things. True lovers of God don't love "prosperity" with all their hearts, souls, and minds. They love "the Lord their God" with all their hearts, souls, and minds.

God's commandments are simple, but to get them to work for you, the conditions are that you know the laws and want to obey them. I love Philippians 2:13 in The Living Bible. *"For God is at work within you, helping you want to obey him, and then helping you do what he wants."* Simple, isn't it? But you must want God more than things before you can enjoy the things God gives you.

Let's go back to Deuteronomy 28:20, 21 TLB for just a minute:

> *For the Lord himself will send his person-*

*al curse upon you. You will be confused
and a failure in everything you do, until at
last you are destroyed because of the sin
of forsaking him. He will send disease
among you until you are destroyed from
the face of the land which you are about
to enter and possess.*

God had just preceded this with a condition.
*"If you won't listen to the Lord your God and
won't obey these laws I am giving you today,
then all of these curses shall come upon you."*
God is saying to us, stick with him and his
abundant ways and we will prosper, but if we
don't want to prosper, then we can expect his
laws to work against us.

Remember, we are talking about the conditions of prosperity. We are actually making
a choice ourselves as to whether we want prosperity or poverty. We are learning some of the
conditions that will enable us to live in the
abundance Jesus promised us. All we have to
do is do the simple things God and Jesus instructed us to do, and God's word will work at
all times. We must constantly seek God in his
word and in our talking and thinking with
him. Seek God and you will find him, and then
you will have all the prosperity of all kinds.
That's a big promise, isn't it?

Deuteronomy 28:27-29 TLB says,

*He will send upon you Egyptian boils, tu-
mors, scurvy, and itch, for none of which
will there be a remedy. He will send mad-
ness, blindness, fear, and panic upon you.
You shall grope in the bright sunlight just
as the blind man gropes in darkness. You
shall not prosper in anything you do...*

That's a promise of God that you will not
prosper under the conditions that you disobey
his laws. But, look at our choice in Deuteronomy 29:9 TLB. This is the will of God; this is
the prosperity of God: *"Therefore, obey the
terms of this covenant so that you will prosper
in everything you do."*

I think it is so wonderful of God to leave
us with a simple choice of living in his abundant prosperity or living in miserable poverty.
I like prosperity better, don't you?

Chapter Six

Prosperity During Tough Times

David was a man after God's own heart who loved to obey God's laws and who meditated day and night in them that he might know all God wanted him to do. Join him in his wisdom and understanding of God and God's desire for our prosperity as he begins Psalm 1:1, 2 TLB.

> *Oh, the joys of those who do not follow evil men's advice, who do not hang around with sinners, scoffing at the things of God: But they delight in doing every-thing God wants them to, and day and night are always meditating on his laws and thinking about ways to follow him*

more closely.

They are like trees along a river bank bearing luscious fruit each season without fail. Their leaves shall never wither, and all they do shall prosper.

David was living in prosperity. He knew what God wanted, and he wanted what God knew was best for him. He wasn't trying to get from God; he was wanting to do for God.

Blessed is the man that walketh not in the counsel of the ungodly. If you don't listen to sinners tell you how to become prosperous, then God can prosper you. That's a condition of prosperity. We are to keep our eyes on the promises of God, his instructions, his counsel if we want his prosperity.

That doesn't mean that businessmen or women who have trained themselves in a trade or profession aren't to be consulted by you. Many doctors, lawyers, accountants, computer experts, and others who know their business are not Christians but are worthy of listening to for advice from the facts they know. But when it comes to things of God, and his laws and principles, then go only to God or his people who know him for counsel. Obedience to his laws will bring prosperity, and we must be careful where we go to find the meaning of his laws.

If we will find our counsel by meditating in the word of God many hours daily, finding ways to please him and principles he writes on our hearts as we meditate, his laws become a part of us and will bring all manner of prosperity. Those who meditate on his laws day and night shall be like trees along a river bank bearing luscious fruit each season without fail. The leaves and lives of those who do this shall never wither, and all they do shall prosper. What a condition for us to follow, meditating in his word day and night. I love to spend hours and hours meditating in the Bible, and it really brings forth fruit and prosperity in my life, and it will in yours, too.

When God said, "Let there be light," light appeared. God spoke into being a force, an energy that never stops unless he stops it. When God speaks a law, it continues to have a force that will bring action. When God said that if we would obey his laws we would prosper, then it has to be so. We will prosper.

God didn't say he would overflow our bank accounts with excess money. He did say, "I will supply all your needs when you do what I say." Actually we are working for Jesus and he pays well for our services when we do our job. He didn't say he would feed us steak ten times a day; he said he would supply all our needs. All our needs are those things which are necessary for us to perform his word while we are on earth. He will not supply our needs to disobey him. He will supply our needs to obey him and carry on his plans. That is a condition God wisely places on us so that we will live in all of his abundant prosperity. He thinks bigger than we do.

If we try to leave out part of God's message or twist it to fit our desires instead of his, then we are not able to call upon God to perform his word. Sometimes we try to use our desires and attitudes to make God disobey his laws for our benefits by trying to command God to obey one of his promises. We can let God know we know his promises (and he already knows that) and God delights in performing his word when we do that. God will even answer our prayers before we pray if we are fulfilling his conditions. He loves to bless those who bless him.

One of the great promises of prosperity with a condition is found in Matthew 6:8-15. I'm going to use the Amplified Bible for this because it expands the meaning a little, and also I want you to start before the Lord's model prayer and continue after it. Note the conditions (or the laws of God) for him to perform this beautiful prayer:

"Do not be like them, for your Father

knows what you need before you ask Him."
Isn't that powerful! That's abundance in prosperity.

"Pray therefore like this: Our Father Who is in heaven, hallowed (kept holy) be Your name. Your kingdom come, Your will be done, on earth as it is in heaven." God really lives like a king in heaven. He has pure transparent gold by the tons. Probably uses pure gold plates or whatever we will use for our banquet when we get there. And yet, he says that his will for us is the same on earth as it is in heaven.

> *Give us this day our daily bread* [In Philippians 4:19 KJV, Paul says,] *"But my God shall supply all your need according to his riches in glory by Christ Jesus."* *And forgive us our debts, as we also have forgiven* [left, remitted and let go the debts, and given up resentment against] *our debtors.*

> *And lead* [bring] *us not into temptation, but deliver us from the evil one. For Yours is the kingdom and the power and the glory forever. Amen.*

> *For* [watch for the conditions of prosperity] *if you forgive people their trespasses*

> *—that is, their reckless and willful sins, leaving them, letting them go and giving up resentment—your heavenly Father will also forgive you.*
>
> *But if you do not forgive others their trespasses—their reckless and willful sins, leaving them, letting them go and giving up resentment—neither will your Father forgive you your trespasses.*

We often expect God to give us our daily bread, pay our bills, keep the enemy from causing sickness or robbing us of success, but do we always look at the conditions of examining our attitudes to see if we are obeying all of his commandments? Many recite the word of God expecting him to fill our bank accounts with money and our garages with cars, when we have not hearkened to the voice of the Lord our God to do all he has commanded us to do, including forgiving those who wrong us or hurt us.

But when we do all his commandments and forgive those who have sinned against us, then we can expect his kingdom on earth to be prosperous like the one in heaven. It's going to get "gooder" and "gooder" as we learn more and more how to make his kingdom work on earth. The earth is good and is a great place to

live, and we should be living in a modern
garden of Eden. God wants that for us.

Praise God, we don't have to worry about
what happens to our economy when we are operating in the realm of God's laws. Bread will
go to $20 a loaf according to the Living Bible
in Revelation 6:6, but that should be after we
are in heaven with the Bread of Life. But whatever the price of bread or other food and cloth-
ing, God said that if we would obey all his
commandments, he would supply all our need
according to his riches in glory by Christ Jesus.
That means he will! I don't know whether I
will have the cash to pay the grocer for all my
needs, but I do know that God will provide a
way that his righteous will never be forsaken
nor his seed out begging for bread.

He may even require us to go on a fast for
him to provide our needs, but that's all right.
He may require us to live on one meal a day,
but if so that is all we need to maintain perfect
health and strength. I don't know how he will
do it, but this one thing I know—he will do it.
All I know is that Frances and I trust God, and
we hope you do, too. He is perfectly reliable
and in fact is the only stable thing in existence.

Abraham trusted God, and he had all his
needs supplied. Joseph trusted God, and he
had all his needs supplied.

Jesus is the same yesterday, today, and

forever, so why should we worry if we are
children of God and doing what he said for us
to do?

It's exciting to know that we don't have to
be operating in poverty when God promises
prosperity. His conditions are so simple and
are worth it all. Sometimes he requires a lot of
us, but he always comes through gloriously if
we keep trusting him. Jacob worked seven
years for his lover, Rachel, and then was de-
ceived and had to work another seven years to
get the abundant prosperity he wanted. That
not only took faith, but it took a lot of sweat.

God often requires a lot from us so that
our faith and trust in him will be prosperity to
him. He deserves to be prosperous, too. We
make God prosperous by continuing to work
for him and trust him, no matter what happens. Some of his conditions to work for him
are to work hard, produce good results in our
labor, work six days a week, use common
sense, use good judgment, work diligently,
love our neighbor and our boss as ourselves,
trust God with all our hearts and lean not on
our own understanding; trust God when things
don't seem right, and on and on. But all those
things seem trivial when compared to the security found in trusting God and his return system.

We must watch all of the Bible conditions
and do them in order for them to work for us.

One man told us the other day that he had been sitting around waiting for four months for God to supply proper food for his family. He wouldn't work because, he said, "I claim God's promise of supplying all my needs." God said a lot more than that, and that man let his family go hungry, which certainly is not God's way of doing things. He just sat down and became poverty-stricken. God's laws worked for him—God said that is what would happen if we disobeyed his laws. He tried to take one verse and squeeze God into it to obtain a selfish desire.

You can't do it that way. You must obey *all* of God's laws. You must meditate in his laws day and night so that you will understand what he wants to do for us when we do what he wants. Nobody wants us to prosper more than God.

The devil wants to put poverty and sickness on us, but if we are walking in God's prosperity, he cannot succeed. He is defeated by the word of God. In Isaiah 54:17 God says:

> *No weapon that is formed against you shall prosper; and every tongue that accuses you in judgment you will condemn. This is the heritage of the servants of the Lord* (NASB).

Do you see that God's prosperity overcomes the devil's poverty and sickness? We win. But we still must walk in the will and ways of God, or the devil has a right to put curses on us. We can operate in either prosperity or poverty. We can walk in God's ways or the devil's.

We who walk in the ways of God are heirs of salvation; that means heirs of all of God's prosperity. Salvation includes finances, health, and all other good things of God.

The more of this book I write from the word of God, the more foolish it appears to choose the devil's way to slide into poverty when God makes it so plain what he wants to do for us.

I can just hear God say, Charles and Frances, your cupboard is a little low, so why don't you walk up on that hill over yonder? That's a piece of my property, and you can use anything you find there. It all belongs to my family, so help yourself. There is a large herd of cattle, some deer and antelope, some wild turkeys, and a lot of other things. There is a spring up near the top and there are all kinds of vegetables and fruit, so help yourselves. By the way, if you will take a pan with you, there's a lot of fresh water fish in the spring lake, so why not enjoy some of it while you are up there, and bring all you want back with you? When you get through cooking the fish, why don't you dip the pan into the gravel in the bottom of that stream? I have stored so much gold there that you can get all you need to make any purchases you desire.

Oh, yes, and if anyone stops you and says, why are you doing this, just say, "The Lord has need of it!" (See Mark 11:3). If he tries to give you any trouble, just tell him your God owns the cattle on a thousand hills and this is one of his hills. He also owns not only the surface rights, but all the mineral rights, too.

Now, don't get the idea from this that God says to go gather your neighbor's crops.

Our Father is very rich, and as his children we have inherited all of his kingdom. Of course, we still are required to do what God says, or else he has to restrict us to protect us from the curses of the law. That's double prosperity.

Peter was a man who succeeded, even though he had some problems along the way. After he received the baptism with the Holy Spirit, he never wavered from obeying and trusting God. He is in heaven now and what greater prosperity than that can we ever desire?

Then Peter answered and said to Him, "Behold, we have left everything and fol-

lowed You; what then will there be for us?"

And Jesus said to them, "Truly I say to you, that you who have followed Me, in the regeneration when the Son of Man will sit on His glorious throne, you also shall sit upon twelve thrones, judging the twelve tribes of Israel.

"And everyone who has left houses or brothers or sisters or father or mother or children or farms for My name's sake, shall receive many times as much, and shall inherit eternal life" (Matthew 19:27-29 NASB).

Do you see the fantastic prosperity promises Jesus has made to us in those verses? What are his conditions? First, he identified those to whom he was giving his best as the ones who follow him, first the disciples, then anyone who has left those whom he loves most and things he values.

Those who follow him by *giving everything,* like the disciples of old and those of us today, are the ones to whom he will give the prosperity in full. Those who give up personal loves *for his name's sake* is another of the conditions for these great rewards. How much are

we going to receive when we meet these conditions for prosperity? *Many times* as much as
we give. *And* eternal life besides. Is that
generous prosperity? That doesn't mean God
is going to strip you of everything good on
earth if you don't go off preaching some-
where. But his condition does mean that you
put him absolutely first while you are working
at your job.

What is more valuable, those whom we
love and the things of this earth of value, *or*
many times as much love for those we love and
many times more things of this earth of value?
It still looks foolish not to accept the offers of
God and Jesus instead of the poverty and
curses which will come if we don't. What do
we have to lose if we ignore the promises and
conditions? Everything, including eternal life
in the most glorious home ever conceived, our
heavenly home with God, Jesus, vast hosts of
angels and multiplied numbers of friends who
are there. Hallelujah! I'll stay on the winning
side. How about you?

Perhaps a scripture that Frances loves and
uses most is Luke 6:38, and she reads it mostly
from the King James version, so let's look at it
with her to see what God has to offer.

> *Give, and it shall be given unto you; good
> measure, pressed down, and shaken togeth-*

*er, and running over, shall men give into
your bosom. For with the same measure
that ye mete withal it shall be measured to
you again.*

This is the prosperity reward. But where do we
find the conditions for all that to become
ours? There is so much in the Bible that is so
good that I just want to keep telling you more
and more from the word. I have found that the
only true source of the abundance, the ever-
present happiness and joy, the peace of God
that always exists no matter how bad the situations are around me, comes from hundreds of
places in the Bible. I love the things God has
given us and I love to obey his wishes. What
looks hard when we hesitate to do what God
says actually is very easy when we really, truly
want to forget ourselves and do what he wants.

To find the real conditions of Luke 6:38's
riches, look at the conditions that came before
the blessings. From The Living Bible, verses 22
and 23, for example:

*What happiness it is when others hate you
and exclude you and insult you and smear
your name because you are mine! When
that happens, rejoice! Yes, leap for joy!
For you will have a great reward awaiting
you in heaven. And you will be in good*

*company—the ancient prophets were
treated that way too!*

On the surface, being hated, excluded, and in-
sulted doesn't sound like prosperity. But Jesus
said it was, when it was done because you did
it for him.

In Luke 6:36-38 TLB Jesus says:

*Try to show as much compassion as your
Father does. Never criticize or con-
demn—or it will all come back on you.
Go easy on others; then they will do the
same for you. For* [now comes the reward
if you meet those conditions] *if you give
you will get! Your gift will return to you
in full and overflowing measure, pressed
down, shaken together to make room for
more, and running over. Whatever measure you use to give—large or small—will
be used to measure what is given back to
you.*

Do you see what I mean by the conditions
which bring prosperous blessings? God set
principles that work; he established laws that
work perfectly. It's up to us to flow with those
principles. No airplane could fly if the engi-
neers and designers had not discovered the
principles of aerodynamics that cause those

tons of weight to move upward. They discovered that by the proper shape of wings they could cause a vacuum to form over the wings as the plane moved along the ground or through the air. They found out that if they did that, the plane would lift, actually pulled up by a vacuum.

When the turbulence disturbs that flow with the laws of aerodynamics, this lift will be stopped or changed. They discovered that they needed this law, too, or else the plane would keep on lifting and they could never land it or change its direction. They obeyed God's laws which he made perfect when he created air.

Jesus said that when turbulence comes, like men hating you and excluding you and insulting you, take advantage of his law and you can control the situation. He said that when turbulence comes like that, rejoice. Yes, leap for joy! Do you see why he established that rejoicing principle at a time of distress? He wanted to keep you calm instead of distressed, so he set up the law of trust in him. "Peace, be still," Jesus said when the storms came up. "Relax and trust me. Have faith that I will take care of you when you are helpless to do anything about the circumstances of life."

God's laws keep lifting you up no matter how heavy the weight you feel on your shoulders. "Trust me. Trust me. Trust me. Don't let turbulence stop your trusting in me. Peter, keep your eyes off the stormy waves and keep them on me, then you can walk on water. You can walk on top of those problems. You can rejoice and leap for joy while they are happening. Not because the circumstances seem prosperous, but because my provision is always there if you trust me."

Criticizing and complaining take you into the cursing side of the law. Your reaction to someone else criticizing you and complaining against you will determine whether you are receiving God's prosperity or the devil's poverty. The law Jesus stated was that we are not to criticize and complain. Why not obey his laws and receive his blessings pressed down, shaken together and running over? When you react to criticism and complaining by others with love, this puts you on the receiving end of blessings. If you criticize and complain, you lose. Criticism and complaining will be given unto you, pressed down, shaken together, and running over. Be sure to give what God designed and not what the devil steals, and then you benefit from the blessings God promises.

Jesus is our model of life. If we could live exactly as he did, there would never be a more successful life. He had a hard condition to meet, but he did it because he always trusted his Father. God has designed a plan of redemption for all mankind, a plan for our eternal prosperity. His plan was that Jesus should come to earth, give up his great riches in heaven, be persecuted, be killed, so that he through his resurrection could bring salvation to all of us. Jesus had a choice. Would he meet God's conditions or would he fail to trust God?

> *You know how full of love and kindness our Lord Jesus was: though he was so very rich, yet to help you he became so very poor, so that by being poor he could make you rich* (II Corinthians 8:9 TLB).

Could anything be more plainly stated than that promise of God? Jesus fully made the provision for riches for us instead of poverty. He did all that is needed by him. He provided not only for us to be rich, but to be in health. *"Beloved, I wish above all things that thou mayest prosper and be in health, even as thy soul prospereth"* (III John 2 KJV). The condition Jesus was required to meet was met; now he is saying, get your soul lined up, let it be healthy and prosper, and *then* my provisions of prosperity and health can come to you.

> *But if anyone keeps looking steadily into God's law for free men, he will not only remember it but he will do what it says,*

and God will greatly bless him in every-
thing he does (James 1:25 TLB).

Condition: keep looking steadily into God's
law, then do what it says and you will be
blessed with prosperity in everything you do.
Is that fair enough? Sounds good to me.

Do you consider *love* prosperity?

If you believe that Jesus is the
Christ—that he is God's Son and your
Savior—then you are a child of God. And
all who love the Father love his children
too. So you can find out how much you
love God's children—your brothers and
sisters in the Lord—by how much you
love and obey God. Loving God means
doing what he tells us to do, and really,
that isn't hard at all; for every child of
God can obey him, defeating sin and evil
pleasure by trusting Christ to help him (I
John 5:1-3 TLB).

God makes abundance so available to us and
so plain that we really have no reason not to
live in his prosperity of love all the time. The
worst thing I can think of that hell is like is
that there is absolutely no love there. The best
thing heaven has to offer is perpetual, overwhelming love, for God is love and he is there.

What are the conditions for prosperity in love?
Find out through loving your brothers and sis-
ters in Christ how much you love and obey
God.

How much did our model Jesus love? He
loved the maximum by giving his life for us, so
that we can have life and have it more abundantly.

Jesus could have stayed in heaven with all
the glory of God and riches beyond measure,
but he obeyed God. While he was on earth, he
could have had the whole world if he had wor-
shiped Satan just a little bit, but he obeyed
God. He could have called twelve legions of
angels to save him from the cross, but he
obeyed God. He knew that he would even be
separated from God, that his very eternal soul
would go into hell and be subject to Satan's
power, but he obeyed God. He knew that upon
his return to heaven with all the sins of the
world on his shoulders, his own Father would
turn his back to him because God cannot look
at sin, but he obeyed God. He fulfilled all that
God asked him to do for you and me and now
Jesus sits at the right hand of his Father, enjoying all the glory that could have been lost to
him, but he was more concerned for you and
me that we might be his glory.

Because of Jesus and his obedience to
God, we can have abundance of peace, joy,

riches, health, and all the other ingredients of prosperity. What an exciting day that will be when we look up and see our redemption drawing near. When we see Jesus coming down from heaven for the second time to receive us and take us to his glory and our glory in heaven with God.

Chapter Seven

Prosperity in Marriage

Prosperity is lacking in marriages probably more than in any other place. A majority of couples living together today are marriage-poor, and poverty-stricken conditions exist in marriages because of a lack of understanding of what is possible for all of us.

If you wrote on a piece of paper all the ways you could imagine that would make your marriage prosperous, what would you list?

- Communication so perfect and faultless that you would enjoy every moment with your spouse.
- Companionship so loving, understanding, and tender that you would have

perfect peace every moment you are together.

- Sex so perfect that you would live in a state of blissful satisfaction at all times.
- A home that was exactly what you and your spouse would consider perfect, whether it be a cottage by the sea, or a mansion in the mountains.
- Security so totally complete that you would never be concerned about money, clothes, or any of the nice things of life.
- Togetherness so complete that you could hardly stand leaving your spouse even to go to work.
- The best looking husband or the most beautiful wife you could possibly imagine.
- Retirement while you are young enough to enjoy it and enough money that you could continually do anything you would like.
- Complete freedom from all responsibilities of life.
- Perfect health at all times for you and your spouse.
- A big family of healthy, happy children.

This list could go on and on until it got longer than a mail order catalog that lists everything anyone could want or need.

If you had everything you listed, and even more than that, all directed toward making your marriage perfect, would you have complete success and total prosperity in your union with your mate? Let me ask you a few questions:

• What does it take to have prosperity in your marriage?
• What is prosperity in marriage?
• Can everyone who is married have prosperity?

The answer very simply is "Yes" if you meet God's conditions, because God wants only the very best for his family.

Can you picture yourself at the weddings of your children? What would you honestly wish for them? That everything in their marriages would be the very best—or would you wish that their marriages would be miserable? Can you picture in the same way God, our eternal Father, saying , "I'm going to use all of my power to make you miserable all your life?"

God has proven himself totally and completely a God of love, and he has shown for thousands of years his great patience in trying to get mankind to love him back. He created us for intimate fellowship with him. He needs us.

God made marriage to be the most exact replica of our relationship with Jesus that he could possibly make. A perfect relationship with our spiritual husband, Jesus, leads to the abundant, overflowing life that is promised in the Word of God. We are instructed to love our neighbors as much as we love ourselves and to love God more than we love anybody or anything. Then he goes further in the fifth chapter of Ephesians to show how much love and respect he wants husbands and wives to give to their spouses. Within this realm lies perfection in marriage to the exact degree we are willing to fully meet his conditions for a prosperous marriage.

Actually, as good and godly as all those things are that you or I listed, they still do not fit the conditions that God gives for the most abundant life we could have. God's laws and conditions are very plain and clear in the Bible. They are simple and easy to obey, and they are effortless to discover if you want to obey them. But they are most obscure to find, and most laborious to obey if you don't want to do what God wants you to do.

I always like to go back to the very foundation, the very root of all the principles of what God wants of his people. The foundation started even before God made the earth as we know it. It all started in heaven.

God and Jesus are the only ones who are so perfect that they can be the highest rulers, total monarchs, and can still not have pride of self. When their total nature, their Spirits, are within us, then their perfect nature can also rule our lives and make us capable of being rulers without pride of self.

In heaven God is all in all, and his Son Jesus is his exact likeness. God created a great host, possibly billions, of angels to make heaven a perfect and beautiful environment. He made them so perfect that they would be in the high position of serving every need of the most high God forever.

He made Lucifer one of his most beautiful angels. Lucifer was in one of the highest positions of honor and was very close to the throne of God. Everything was so perfect and he was so perfect that it is impossible to comprehend with our finite minds or even wildly imagine anything so prosperous. He had all the prosperity even God could provide. Why didn't he continue in this position of abundant prosperity?

He failed to meet God's conditions. He let *self* be exalted. *Pride of self* entered into his heart. He allowed a desire to creep in to please *self* more than he wanted to serve and please

God. That is probably why God put the first commandment right in front of the other nine that he gave to the Israelites, *"You shall have no other gods before Me"* (Exodus 20:3 NASB).

You might think, "I wonder how long it took for the *self* desire to build up within Lucifer?" God knows all things, and he cannot stand sin. The Bible doesn't say, but I believe that the very moment, at the very microsecond the thought or even the intent entered the mind of Satan (Lucifer), God knew all about it and, without hesitation, threw Satan out of heaven like a bolt of lightning. God's laws of prosperity and abundance will not function in an atmosphere where *self* exists.

You might say, "Well, how can God be so exalted if he doesn't want *self* to be exalted?" God's total nature is love, and love always wants to give itself away. God, the supreme head over all human beings and of everything ever made, is the very greatest of servants. His whole being—his nature and his character—wants to give himself and his abundant prosperity away all the time.

Because Adam and Eve allowed sin to enter in, every life created from them, including each of us, is born with the sinful nature of the devil. That characteristic is the same one that entered into Lucifer in heaven—*self*. Adam and Eve in their perfect life of abundance and completeness very simply chose *self-pleasure* more than trusting God, and *self* destroyed all their prosperity.

It is quite obvious, then, that *we must self-destruct* to be created a new, prosperous person. That doesn't mean physical suicide. It simply means your selfish desires must totally die and in their place we must put total trust in God and his promises. Giving up self is easy, if we sincerely and unreservedly want the abundant life Jesus promised to those who would obey God. We must determine in our hearts that we are going to put forth all the effort and work necessary to find out what pleases God instead of self and then do without reservation whatever God wants. God's power is necessary to enable us to do that, but his power is ever abundantly available if we faithfully serve him. In fact, he makes his power so easily accessible to us that he fills our very spirits with himself. The greatest power plant on earth is in you and me when we are filled with the Holy Spirit.

With these principles of God's conditions for prosperity in mind, let us carefully and intimately examine marriage and see how to attain perfection in it. First of all, it takes two individuals working together. You can no more have a perfect marriage with only one spouse wanting to blend with God's laws than you can have a perfect running automobile with half the spark plugs missing from the engine.

Not all marriages have two people with a mutual desire to please God. However, even one spouse can do a lot for the marriage if he or she follows God's laws. Following God is not easy, but it will help, and perhaps the other spouse will eventually see the blessings that come when we live God's way. Frances and I receive a lot of testimonies telling how husbands or wives saw tremendous change in their spouses when they started trusting Jesus, and, as a result, they themselves accepted Jesus and the marriage was healed.

In many ways Frances and I have just as ordinary conditions in our home life as anyone else. Some of the conditions are different because we are constantly busy in full-time work for Jesus. But we have days at home when we live like a typical family. We have discovered that whether we are out of the city or at home working in the business end of our ministry, we are still the same two people, and God is the same God and his laws are the same laws.

Most people have never discovered that *you can never get away from yourself,* so be happy and search for ways to make life a success where you are. Remember, your problems will follow *you* wherever you go, and so will your blessings.

Let's take the first item I listed for ways to make your marriage prosperous (not that it is necessarily the most important one).

Communications

We often say that we talk about Jesus all the time, so there is no shortage of stimulating conversation and exciting communication. We briefly discuss what we will have for breakfast or supper, but this is a quickly finished subject on which we spend a minimum of time.

Because Jesus is the center and the very heart of our lives, our marriage, and our home, he is the center and the very heart of our conversation.

The Bible says to pray continually. Years ago I thought, "I can't pray five minutes without running out of something to say to God." Then I learned a great secret which keeps the line of communication with God open at all times.

In my professional life as a certified public accountant, I was very conscientious and loyal to my clients. I worked diligently to make everything I did for them a total success. I had hundreds of clients and each one was very special to me, but I didn't just think about their work when I was with them or working for them.

I always planned the next day's work long before the previous day ended. I knew which client I would be working for, and I knew exactly what I was to do for them. Because my heart was a giving heart in business, I thought through their needs during my off-work time. In fact, the time I did my most productive and creative thinking was early in the morning while I was shaving, bathing, and getting ready for the day's work. I carefully and painstakingly analyzed each and every situation.

If they had a tax problem, I would let my mind examine alternatives. I would think, "If I do thus and so, we will get the best possible tax advantage, or maybe we can do it this way and even get better and more choice benefits." Then I would probe into the area of the risks we would take if we did the tax planning some other way. By meditating in this manner I was able to think through many situations and alternatives and then go to my tax laws and reference books to prove the best way. After that, my clients and I would make decisions.

After I yielded my life totally to God and to Jesus and was meditating in the Word of God almost day and night for about a year, the principles of God's laws were so ingrained in my mind and written on my heart that they infiltrated every thought and every decision I made.

One morning while I was shaving and thinking through a client's needs, I discovered a remarkable secret that changed my life in the area of communications.

I discovered that instead of thinking to myself, I was *thinking to God*.

I would think, "God, if I apply this tax law to their situation, will that mean that I can get the best tax advantage, or if I do it this way, will that be better? Will I be risking losing more benefits if I do it this way, or should I take the less risky route?"

I discovered that by filtering my thoughts through God, his mighty Spirit would alert my mind to things I knew and direct my thoughts to the best and most prosperous way to benefit my clients. God was vitally interested in giving me his best, if I would think to him and let him guide me. Because I wanted to please God, he caused me to do a far greater job in pleasing my clients.

Sometimes my mind sent signals like a thousand little thoughts searching outward for answers and alternatives, and then they all came back into my mind as though through a funnel. God directed my mind in my everyday affairs and decisions.

At about five o'clock one Sunday morning I discovered one of God's laws, which helped explain my thinking to God and God thinking back to me in making decisions.

God had just appointed Saul to be king of Israel, but Saul was really not trained to be king. He didn't know how to make all the decisions and to make wise judgment in ruling this vast nation of people. He became king, and God's prophet, Samuel, was to anoint him so that the Holy Spirit would be upon him. Samuel poured a flask of oil over Saul. That was symbolic of pouring the Spirit of God on him.

Right after the anointing, in I Samuel 10:6, 7 a law or condition of God was given that exploded in my spirit when I discovered it.

> *At that time the Spirit of the Lord will come mightily upon you, and you will prophesy with them and you will feel and act like a different person. From that time on your decisions should be based on whatever seems best under the circumstances, for the Lord will guide you.* (TLB).

I had always made decisions based on whatever seemed best under the circumstances. I had carefully considered all conditions and alternatives before making decisions.

But God said something I hadn't discovered in his laws before. He said *he would guide us* if we followed after his Holy Spirit, his ways, his desires. He would direct our daily lives and decisions.

Glory to God, he will guide all of us in our daily decisions if we will trust him, learn his laws and conditions and then obey them. Trusting God works.

And it will work in communicating with our spouse in marriage. If we are constantly talking about ways we can bless God through doing what he wants us to do, he will give us more to talk about than we have time to say. Frances and I often say, "Oh, I forgot to tell you thus and so!" It is because we have so much to talk about that we don't remember to tell each other all the little things of possible interest or minor importance.

Yes, we have prosperity in communications in our marriage, and you can, too—if you will search God's promises in his Word and then want to do what pleases him. He will keep you busy, and you will never be bored and lacking something good to talk about to your beloved.

Companionship

Jesus said to love your neighbor as yourself. Then in Ephesians 5:25 (TLB) he said:

> *"And you husbands, show the same kind of love to your wives as Christ showed to the church when he died for her."* Verse 28: *"That is how husbands should treat their wives, loving them as parts of themselves. For since a man and his wife are now one, a man is really doing himself a favor and loving himself when he loves his wife!"*

If you are irritated by something your spouse did, right or wrong, you will be tempted to cut him or her down with unkind words or even argue or fight over who is right or wrong. God says to treat your spouse just like you treat yourself and, even more importantly, like you treat Jesus.

Because I love Frances, if I say something cutting or bad to or about her, I must look up to Jesus and say, "Jesus, that goes for you, too!" And I must say it with the same attitude I say it to Frances. But the good part is that when I tell Frances how perfect and how beautiful she is, I can say to Jesus, "That goes for you, too!"

Jesus said, *"...to the extent that you did it to one of these brothers of Mine, even the least of them, you did it to Me"* (Matthew 25:40 NASB).

If your communication is always directed by the laws of God, then you will have companionship so precious and enjoyable that you will want to be with that companion all the time. Frances and I are together almost twenty-four hours every day of every year, and we never grow tired of one another. When we have been apart even for a few minutes or a few hours, we always rush back into each other's arms.

That's prosperity in companionship.

Why is our companionship so perfect? Because we have meditated on God's conditions night and day with the sole purpose of pleasing God and Jesus, and their laws work in our favor by giving us the same companionship that exists between God and Jesus. Can you imagine God getting tired of living with Jesus? We should never let the things of our daily life make us tired of pleasing one another.

Sex

Is your sex life in your marriage prospering?

God created this culmination of love in his first creatures, and he wants this to be a thrilling part of our earthly lives. His laws and conditions work beautifully in the sex area of marriage, just as they do in every other area, to bring the ultimate prosperity in such an important part of our lives. God wants our sex life to prosper.

We should wholeheartedly want to do everything in our power to please and satisfy our spouse. This is just as much a part of God's conditions for prosperity in sex as the requisite of doing everything in our power to please God and Christ Jesus if we want to have an abundant life.

Keep in mind that you cannot have prosperity in sex outside of marriage because that is in violation of God's laws, and when mankind does anything that is contrary to God's laws of sex, he will face eventual failure and utter disappointment and destruction. God highly honors sex in marriage because it is a part of his creation. Because he lives in us as Christians, he will not tolerate any perversion of this body that belongs to him.

> *Don't you realize that all of you together are the house of God, and that the Spirit of God lives among you in his house? If anyone defiles and spoils God's home,*

*God will destroy him. For God's home is
holy and clean, and you are that home* (I
Corinthians 3:16, 17 TLB).

Love is like a thread that weaves our lives as
husband and wife to one another. It is the
bond that makes us one. Just as God and Jesus
are one, so husband and wife are made one
when joined together in marriage under the
laws of God.

Love is an energy that flows between husband and wife. It is more than an attitude,
thing, or relationship. It is alive and powerful.
It is life. Love is alive because God is love and
he is alive.

We can even see a similarity between the
love we give to God and the human love between husband and wife. Love has feeling, but
it is a feeling different than any other feeling in
the human body. When young or old fall deeply in love, something indescribable flows between them.

In Revelation 2:4 (TLB), Jesus said
through John:

*"Yet there is one thing wrong; you don't
love me as at first! Think about those
times of your first love [how different
now!] and turn back to me again and
work as you did before..."*

When that first love is released within God's laws, it can always and continuously be as excitingly fresh as the first flicker that flipped your heart with your true lover.

If your sex life is not prospering, apply this law of God to turn back to Jesus again and work as you did before. Look back to your first love with your spouse and examine what made it so thrilling and enjoyable. Constant care and attention to your spouse are necessary to keep that first love alive year after year. Think back and see if you didn't give tenderness and love generously to your spouse. And remember when you loved him or her so much, their response to you was the love that thrilled your heart.

"Turn back to me again and work as you did before..." Turn back to your beautiful spouse again and work as you did before, and see if your love won't be the same as before. You will discover something else fantastic—the longer you are together applying these laws of love, the greater your love life and your sex life will become.

Don't let your love grow cold toward one another. Work at it, and your effort will return in bountiful measure.

What causes love to grow cold and sex to become either not possible, not enjoyable, or not frequent?

Your sex relationship with one another will be very closely related to your spiritual relationship with God and Jesus. When you are spiritually healthy, happy, and in love with them, you will be so because you have done everything at all times to please them and to obey their laws and conditions for total prosperity. You don't do it to get prosperity—you do it to give prosperity. When you give to God, he prospers, and in turn you prosper. The more you give to God, the more he will give back to you, and he will outgive you every time.

So will your spouse. I could never really receive love from Frances unless I first gave love to her. It is like you have to empty yourself before you have room to receive from others. Love given from our heart to bless our spouse is a living love; it cannot be artificial. Genuine love given will spontaneously flow back into your own life.

If your passion is released to receive satisfaction for yourself, it will not long continue to be enjoyable. If you love your spouse so much that you want with all that is within you to please him or her, then release that desire in sexual communion and when your spouse is satisfied, you will be more than satisfied.

How often do you meditate in the Word of God just to find more ways to tell God and Jesus you love them? I love to spend at least an hour in the early hours of the morning, often at two, three, or four o'clock in the morning, not trying to study the Bible, but to find words and ways to love God and Jesus. If I miss several mornings doing that, I lose the sharp edge of love for them and the Bible. I have to discipline myself to read and even to direct my attention to loving them.

The same thing applies to love and sex. Unless you give it loving attention it will grow cold. Never lose that "first love" freshness from the heart either for God or for each other.

When you get a beautiful bouquet of fresh flowers, you must care for them, or they will wilt and die.

Your love must continually be cared for or it will wilt and die.

If you don't discipline yourself to constantly stay in the Bible and to constantly seek God and ways to please him, you will lose that intimacy with him.

If you only infrequently love your spouse your love will grow cold and uninteresting. He or she needs constant attention in love—not just in sex. We discuss this a lot more in detail in our book *How to Make Your Marriage Exciting,* but it is important to say it briefly here. Let your love start the minute your eyes open when you awaken in the morning and never stop or slow down until you close them in sleep at night.

When you touch each other tenderly, when you speak kindness and love to one another throughout the day and night, then when you come close together in this cocoon that is the apex of love, you will find that you will want to freely give your love. If you don't love all day, you will find that you will want to take love instead of give it, and that is not the bed of prosperity.

"...freely you received, freely give" (Matthew 10:8 NASB). The power of God is freely given to you when you obey Jesus' instructions to *"Heal the sick, raise the dead, cleanse the lepers, cast out demons; freely you received, freely give."* The blessings of God will flow in your sex life if you *want* to freely give to your spouse. God's laws of prosperity in sex work if we will meet his conditions. Love continually.

Anything that is valuable is worth working for; anything you don't work to get and keep will lose its value to you. Is your prosperity in marriage valuable? Is it worth working to keep? Work becomes the highest form of pleasure when we work to please God, Jesus, or our spouse. Giving becomes the highest form of receiving in our relationship with God and with our marriage partner.

Take a quick look at the other items I listed, plus the ones you listed:

- Home
- Security
- Togetherness
- Attractiveness
- Retirement
- Freedom
- Health
- Family

One scripture rather well sums up how to enjoy the greatest of God's prosperity in all these things: *"But seek ye first the Kingdom of God, and his righteousness; and all these things shall be added unto you"* (Matthew 6:33 KJV).

Frances was a widow with two children when God called her into his service. She loved God and Jesus with all her heart, mind, body, and soul and wanted nothing else in life except to have a mad, wild love affair with them the rest of her life. But when I was being brought into her life she didn't understand how God could continue in the direction he was going with her if she got married. Then God said to her through this one verse, "You have sought me first and put my ways first in everything you do and think, so I am going to add Charles to your life to give you everything you need while on earth."

When God let her know that he was the one who would add all those things necessary to give her total prosperity of the greatest dimension she could dream or imagine, she was willing to accept his ways into prosperity and we were soon married. She didn't understand, but she obeyed God.

I didn't understand what God was doing with my life at that same time, but I was totally and completely submitted to him. When my wife died, I honestly felt that God had a plan for me to be single like he did in Paul's life, but when God spoke to me and told me to marry Frances, I believed God. Abraham believed God and God gave him prosperity. When I believed God, God gave me prosperity far beyond anything I could ever dream or imagine.

God's ways to prosperity work, and they are the only ways that work.

Seek God and you will find him. Seek God and you will find the ultimate in prosperity in every area of your life, including your marriage.

Marriage prosperity is:

- Love
- Joy
- Peace
- Longsuffering
- Kindness
- Goodness

- Faithfulness
- Gentleness
- Self-control

With all this from God, you will have whatever you need to fulfill all of those pleasures of God—abundantly.

Chapter Eight

Desires

If you had the chance to acquire anything you desired, what would you choose? Can anyone on earth be so prosperous that they have anything and everything they desire—at all times? That's a big bank account of prosperity.

God said, *"Delight yourself also in the Lord, And He shall give you the desires of your heart"* (Psalm 37:4 NASB).

Frances and I like to teach the blessings of this verse by saying, "Move the period from the end of the sentence back to where it reads, 'Delight yourself also in the Lord.' When you do everything to please God and Jesus, you are delighting them and therefore you delight yourself in them. Once you give all of yourself to please them, then you can move the period back into its place and God will say to you, *'Delight yourself also in the Lord, and He shall give you the desires of your heart.'* The desires of God will be put into your heart until all you want is to fulfill his desires, then the desires of your heart will prosper because they are not selfish."

In the natural realm, our desires are to benefit ourselves. I remember that after my wife died, I had three cars and could only drive one. I needed money because of the tremendous cost of sickness and loss of work, so my human desire was to get all the money I could to pay bills. I could have sold two of the cars and that would have helped. Actually one of them was a Morris Minor that I had purchased while I was in England, and even before my wife died, I found a nurse in the hospital who did not have a car. I had the car serviced, filled with gasoline, washed, polished, and greased; I changed the oil and did everything I could do to make it perfect. I drove it to this nurse's home, signed the title to her, and gave her the keys. She found it difficult to believe that anyone would do such a thing. I'm sure she wondered what sneaky scheme I had up my sleeve. Through the Word of God, a desire to give was inscribed in my heart and it was manifested in this spontaneous gift. The greatest delight I received was the joy it gave to this English nurse. That was worth far more to me than all the money I could have received from its sale.

God must receive great joy when he sees us respond to the principles he has given to us so we can be blessed. I gave because I wanted to. God gave Jesus to us because he wanted to.

The other car was a very fine Buick that was fairly new and in top condition, with low mileage. My pastor's wife did not have a car, and she needed one. I simply signed the title over to her through the church and handed the keys to her. She was blessed even more because I responded to the giving nature of God, and it pleased him.

You might be interested in knowing that recently a beautiful Cadillac Seville Elegante was driven up to our home, the title was signed over to us, and the keys handed to us. God's desires are to abundantly give to those who love him and serve him.

When God writes his laws of giving into our hearts, those laws and desires are always there. *"...to the extent that you did it to one of these brothers of Mine, even the least of them, you did it to Me"* (Matthew 25:40 NASB).

I do not understand how God causes his prosperity to come to us when we have his desires instead of our own, but some way and always he does. God's Word works.

Chapter Nine

The Joy
of the Lord
Is Your Strength
(Nehemiah 8:10)

That is an unusual verse to describe prosperity.
How can the joy of the Lord actually give us
strength? Think about why God would say
such a thing.

> *I advise you to obey only the Holy Spirit's
> instructions. He will tell you where to go
> and what to do, and then you won't al-
> ways be doing the wrong things your evil
> nature wants you to. For we naturally
> love to do evil things that are just the op-
> posite from the things that the Holy Spirit
> tells us to do; and the good things we want
> to do when the Spirit has his way with us
> are just the opposite of our natural*

> *desires. These two forces within us are constantly fighting each other to win control over us, and our wishes are never free from their pressures* (Galatians 5:16, 17 TLB).

The devil wants us to live in poverty in all areas of our life, but Jesus wants us to prosper.

Some of the strongest tools of the devil are depression, despondency, loneliness, grief, suicide, and fear. These are all negative forces used against our bodies, minds, and spirits to defeat us and to take away all of God's prosperity. They are all of the devil and are brought to us to steal, kill, and destroy us and our relationship with God.

Directly the opposite of those forces is the nature of God which is the positive true force. It centers on the fruit of the Spirit and is very powerful.

I read of an experiment made by five atheistic medical doctors. They wanted to find out what takes place when a person dies.

They had an electronic instrument made that would register 500 negative and 500 positive on a meter. They applied this instrument to a radio signal that was sent around the world, and it registered 9 positive.

This instrument was attached to the brain of a patient who was dying of cancer. They placed a sensitive microphone near her mouth, then went into another room to monitor the response on the instrument as she died.

When the final hour approached, they heard her saying something like: "God, I love you; I praise you. You are the only true God; there is no other God. Thank you Father for being so good to me." On and on she went using the mighty name of God in praise and trust.

The doctors became so intent with what she was saying that they forgot to watch the instrument. Suddenly they heard a clicking noise and their attention turned to the cause of the sound. To their amazement the needle was hitting the 500 positive post and trying to go beyond that.

Then they attached the instrument to a second person who was dying. This time they heard words to the effect that "there is no God; if there was a God I would hate him." He cursed and denied the Almighty God.

They were utterly astonished as they watched the needle go to the 500 negative post and try to go further.

To them, this was a scientific proof that there is power that can be measured from what people believe and say. There was more than just an attitude or thought expressed. There was a power from outside them that was greater than the power of positive thinking, great as that power is.

They discovered that God's commandments, when expressed and believed, produced a measurable flow of energy. They were so touched by the results of this experiment that they all gave their lives to God.

When God said, *"Let there be light,"* he spoke into existence an everlasting light to the universe and gave us light on the earth. That same power of God, when believed and spoken by humans who are filled with the power of God's Holy Spirit, will bring forth measurable results. *"God gives life to the dead and calls into being that which does not exist"* (Romans 4:17 NASB). God gave Jesus all of his power, and Jesus delegated this same power to us who believe.

Frances and I have had the awesome privilege of seeing God do hundreds of miracles of great magnitude through us even though we are ordinary human beings, because God gave us his power and Jesus told us we could command things to happen and they would.

We have seen new parts appear in bodies at our command in the name of Jesus. We watched a thumb that was cut off at the second joint grow out to a full thumb right before the eyes of seventy-five people. It was an awesome spectacle.

We watched an arm about ten inches shorter than the other arm grow out in front of our eyes, the eyes of three medical doctors, and about 1,300 people. All we did was to believe what Jesus said, that we could do the same things he did and even greater things, and use his authority to command this miracle to happen. It happened, and we give him great glory.

Our family doctor completed his examination of my beloved Frances and gave us the disturbing news that she had a greatly enlarged heart and excessively high blood pressure. He instructed her to take it easy and to let him check this again soon. He had X-rayed the heart and had scientific evidence of the enlarged heart and the high blood pressure reading.

A few days later, for no apparent reason, Frances went to bed with a bursting headache. We prayed, but when she received no relief, she took several aspirins. The excruciating pain continued. After twenty-four hours of agony, we called the doctor and he sent her medication to bring the pressure down. But, after three hours of medication, her head was still hurting just as violently.

We were praying about what kind of action we should take when a friend came to our home. She was a technician who had her stethoscope and sphygmomanometer with her. The blood pressure at that time was 225/140. The technician noted the enlarged heart and also stated that she could hear air escaping from it because of an obvious hole in the heart.

Something happened inside of me as I realized the devil was attempting to take the life of my beloved. Then I heard God speak to me, telling me to take authority over the heart. In the name of Jesus, and by the power of the Holy Spirit, I started commanding the heart to reduce to normal size, the hole to be healed and the blood pressure to go down to normal. I continued speaking to her heart with the authority God gave us through Jesus Christ, and at the end of twelve minutes the scientific report was: The blood pressure is normal, 140/80. Instantly the agonizing pain left, and Frances got right out of bed, her usual normal, cheerful self.

Frances returned to the same doctor who had X-rayed her and examined her only a few days before, and he made every heart stress test that could be made. He showed us the previous X-ray and the new one and said, "Look at the old heart which was enlarged, and look now at the new normal size heart." He could find no trace of a hole nor any evidence that there ever had been a hole, and he said the blood pressure was excellent at 140/80. His diagnosis was "Frances, you have the heart of a sixteen-year-old girl." Hallelujah!

This time a Spirit-filled Christian doctor had found scientifically measurable results from a miracle of God. Frances has never had a problem with her heart since then.

God's laws are powerful weapons made available to all of us who believe and apply those laws to attain bountiful prosperity in every area of our lives. God wants us to be healthy.

I have shared these stories for the glory of God to show the power of God given to us human beings on earth to provide strength, health, happiness, and any other needs.

Why is the law of God that says, "The joy of the Lord is your strength" so powerful?

The positive force of God and the negative force of Satan are constantly fighting each other to win control over us. We have the power to submit to either of these forces, but we must make the choice.

We are the ones who decide which force we allow to control us. We can give in to the negative, or we can be drawn by the positive. The positive forces are the power of God and his Word; the negative forces are the violation of God's laws. We can either obey or disobey God's laws and we will see results either way. His laws work and are perfect. When we apply

them, we can bring into action those mighty
forces that can make a scientific measuring de-
vice go toward the positive or negative. We
choose what happens, but we cannot control
what happens except by obedience or disobedience of God's laws.

When circumstances of life, trials, disap-
pointments, or any other problems confront
us, we can resist them and turn to trusting
God, or we can give in to them and become defeated, discouraged, depressed, lonely, and
controlled by other negative forces that come
when we disobey God's Word.

> *Submit therefore to God. Resist the devil
> and he will flee from you. Draw near to
> God and He will draw near to
> you...*(James 4:7, 8 NASB).

> *Be anxious for nothing , but in everything
> by prayer and supplication with thanks-
> giving let your requests be made known to
> God. And the peace of God, which sur-
> passes all comprehension, shall guard
> your hearts and your minds in Christ
> Jesus. Finally, brethren, whatever is true,
> whatever is lovely, whatever is of good re-
> pute, if there is any excellence and if any-
> thing worthy of praise, let your mind
> dwell on these things. The things you have*

learned and received and heard and seen in me, practice these things; and the God of peace shall be with you (Philippians 4:6-9 NASB).

God has given us the formula to drive out those negative powers that take away our strength by taking away our joy and replacing it with sadness, unhappiness, depression, fear, defeat, grief, and loneliness.

Do you notice the lack of energy and strength you have when you are downhearted? Do you also notice how full of energy you are when all is going well and you are full of joy?

Frances and I will not allow anything to take away our joy. Yes, we have as many problems as anyone, and our bodies and minds get overly tired at times. But we know that if we maintain joy at all times, our strength will never wane or fail.

When the negative forces try to come against you, recite the scriptures I gave you and learn many more joy-filled scriptures. Speak them out loud every day and you will discover that speaking God's Word will cause you to lift up your head and praise God, no matter what the circumstances.

The joy of the Lord is your strength.
The joy of the Lord is prosperity.

Chapter Ten

The Cost of Riches

How much does a million dollars cost? What is the spiritual cost of prosperity?

Judas paid thirty pieces of silver for the greatest poverty ever purchased. Jesus gave his life for the greatest prosperity ever purchased.

The prosperity Jesus purchased was the redemption of every single individual, from the first man to the last, who would believe that he gave his life for the forgiveness of sin so that man could live in the presence of God while on earth and eternally in heaven. That is why we are his possession—his glory.

The most important person for whom Jesus gave his life is you.

Judas paid a big price for poverty. He was

a traitor to the Son of God and his pay was mental anguish, which led to suicide and eternal darkness in hell.

What choice do we have for prosperity or poverty?

Jesus came to make us rich.

> *You know how full of love and kindness our Lord Jesus was: though he was so very rich, yet to help you he became so very poor, so that by being poor he could make you rich* (II Corinthians 8:9 TLB).

Suppose one of the wealthiest people in the world today came to you and said, "I want to make you very rich, so here is a cashier's check drawn on my account for $10 million."

God owns everything in heaven and in earth, on the earth, under the earth, and all the stars, planets, suns, and moons, and he gave it all to Jesus, and then made us joint heirs with Jesus—for all of this.

Then Jesus came to earth and became poor so that he could make us rich. Ten million dollars. That's nothing compared with what Jesus has given to us. We are very, very rich when we become a member of this family of God. We share in all the riches of God, the most excellent of which is just to live in the luxurious presence of God and Jesus—here on earth, now, and then in heaven forever and forever. That's prosperity.

We must meet one condition to become a member of this wealthy family of God, but it is so easy that it is almost effortless. Turning down all these riches is very hard.

What is the condition of becoming heir to all of God's riches? How do you get into such a wealthy family to be able to receive all of its benefits?

The first requirement to become a member of this family and enjoy all of God's great riches is to be born into that family. That is the only way you can become a blood child of an earthly family—being born into that family.

Jesus said very clearly that in order to get into the kingdom of God, his family, we must be born again.

It wasn't very difficult or complicated for me to be born. My father planted a sperm or a tiny seed that contained my entire life into the womb of my mother, and through the miracle of propagation God designed, that seed multiplied into cells. When my time in the womb was completed, I was born physically. I became a child of Ed Hunter who produced my life from his own life, and my mother who received this life into herself and nourished and cared for it until that life came forth as a baby. I became a little Hunter when I was born into this family.

When Jesus was born on earth as a man, he went through the same physical process of being born. The only difference was that instead of an earthly man like Joseph planting the seed into the womb of Mary, his mother, God planted the seed containing the life of Jesus. Mary was conceived by the Holy Spirit of God, so the life planted into her womb by God produced the child Jesus. Jesus called God his Father because God was the one who planted this seed containing life into the womb of Jesus' earthly mother. Then how could this same thing happen to us if Jesus said, "You must be born again to inherit life from God."

God is a spirit and the Bible refers to his spirit as the Holy Spirit. Jesus, his Son, is also a spirit. Angels, both good and bad, are spirits. The Bible tells us that we, too, are soul and spirit, housed in human flesh. Our soul and spirit live in our bodies.

When Adam and Eve sinned in the Garden of Eden, their souls died and God's Spirit no longer lived in their spirits to give them life. Their physical bodies continued to live for a great number of years even though they had died spiritually.

To bring back God's life into the human soul and spirit, God sent Jesus to earth to make a provision for this to happen. God breathed life into Adam to make him a living soul, so would God again have to breathe life into us to make our souls live?

This is the way God did it:

God had to have a sperm or seed that contained life, just as the seed or sperm my father gave to produce my life. Where would he find such a phenomenal seed that would produce *life* in the soul of mankind?

Abraham is referred to as the father of the children of Israel. God promised him, and gave him, a son through whom his descendants would be as numerous as the sands of the sea and the stars in the sky. But there was something special about this son God gave to Abraham.

Galatians 3:16 NASB tells us, *"Now the promises were spoken to Abraham and to his seed. He does not say, 'And to seeds,' as referring to many, but rather to one, 'And to your seed,' that is, Christ."*

Remember that it was God's Holy Spirit who planted a seed into the womb of Mary so that Jesus could be born a human being.

That same Holy Spirit plants a seed (the Spirit of Jesus Christ) into the soul and spirit of those who will believe in Jesus and accept this seed like my mother accepted a seed from my father, Ed.

Had my mother decided that she did not

want to have a baby Charles, she could have taken measures to not accept this seed. She could have used a contraceptive, an artificial prevention of the fertilization of the human ovum, often called birth control. But she didn't. She accepted the seed that contained my life.

We have a choice of accepting the seed, or the life of Jesus, from God. We can choose whether we want to serve God or the devil. We don't have three choices—just two. My mother only had two choices—to accept or reject the seed containing my life.

When we decide to accept Jesus, the seed of God, God's seed will be planted into our spirit and we will be born again. Then we can call God our Father just like Jesus did, and we can be a child of God and a brother of Jesus. This is our way of becoming a member of the richest family of all, the family of God.

Look at how clearly this is expressed in 1 John 3:1 (TLB):

> *See how very much our heavenly Father loves us, for he allows us to be called his children—think of it—and we really are! But since most people don't know God, naturally they don't understand that we are his children. Yes, dear friends, we are already God's children, right now, and we*

can't even imagine what it is going to be like later on. But we do know this, that when he comes we will be like him, as a result of seeing him as he really is. And everyone who really believes this will try to stay pure because Christ is pure.

But those who keep on sinning are against God, for every sin is done against the will of God. And you know that he could take away our sins, and that there is no sin in him, no missing of God's will at any time in any way. So if we stay close to him, obedient to him, we won't be sinning either; but as for those who keep on sinning, they should realize this: They sin because they have never really known him or become his.

Oh, dear children, don't let anyone deceive you about this: if you are constantly doing what is good, it is because you are good, even as he is. But if you keep on sinning, it shows that you belong to Satan, who since he first began to sin has kept steadily at it. But the Son of God came to destroy these works of the devil. The person who has been born into God's family does not make a practice of sinning, because now God's life is in him;

> *so he can't keep on sinning, for this new*
> *life has been born into him and controls*
> *him—he has been born again.*

What should I do to be born again?

Jesus is our Savior, so we can simply ask him to forgive our sins, our wrong habits and wrong attitudes, and he will. He will remove them from us as far as the east is from the west, never to be remembered again. Then if we really, truly want Jesus to live in us, to be our way, our truth, and our *life,* we can ask him sincerely and he will come into our spirits, put there as the seed of life by the Spirit of God, just as our earthly father placed life into us by his seed in our mother's womb. Believe that Jesus is the Son of God, that he really did die for the resurrection of our life in him, that he was resurrected from the dead and now lives in glory at the right hand of God the Father.

If you do that simple thing, your spirit will be conceived by the Holy Spirit, and the Spirit of Jesus will merge with your spirit and you will be *born again* spiritually. Glory to God!

If you did that, you are now a member of God's royal family and entitled to all his prosperity. Is that all there is to it? Let's examine that question.

When I was a baby, I didn't have to do anything to be a part of this family. My mother, father, brothers, and sisters did everything for me. They fed me and took care of me.

As I got older, my parents began to give me responsibilities as a part of this family. It took all of us to do all the daily tasks that needed to be done. I then learned to work, and fortunately I learned to enjoy that work. My father and mother told me what my duties were, and they had a way of disciplining me so that whether I wanted to or not, I knew I must do them. My instructions for being a part of this family were clear, and when we all did our part, the family ran smoothly. When one of us didn't do our part, we had problems.

God's conditions for enjoying the benefits and blessings of being a part of this great family of God include many responsibilities and conditions. The interesting thing is that just as each member of our earthly family had to perform their part for the family to prosper in enjoyment and comforts of living, so it is in God's family.

God will always prosper, but we will only prosper to the extent we do our part willingly and joyfully.

We were with our son, Tom, and his family, enjoying the fun of all being in the swimming pool at their home. The four children were playing, diving, splashing, and having a super good time. They got a little rough, and one of them got mad at the others. She went to the end of the pool by herself and pouted for several minutes. She was miserable.

The other kids continued to have a great time, ignoring her. Finally I went over to her, put my arm around her and said, "Look at the others having a good time. Do you notice that you are the only one who is not enjoying the swim?"

That was simple wisdom and love, but she was smart enough to see what I meant, and it was only a few minutes until she was back having fun with the others. When you look at "self" you are always miserable.

We must cooperate with the members of our family and obey the simple laws of loving one another, forgiving one another, overlooking the weaknesses of the others, and many of the other conditions God put into his instructions for prosperity in our homelife.

Our granddaughter was disobeying God's conditions, and she was living for a few minutes in poverty. As soon as she obeyed God's laws, which said to love one another, to forgive those who did you wrong, to be filled with joy, and many other principles God established so we could have prosperity in all things, she again entered into that joyful realm of prosperity.

Did you notice in that simple illustration that God's laws are all for our good? They are never to stop us from having abundant fun or peace or joy. God made every conceivable provision for our enjoyment in everything we do. Satan is the thief who wants to steal the family fortune away from us. He does the most stupid and absurd, yet clever, things to convince us that disobedience to God will benefit us. It never does. Obedience will always benefit us.

What is the cost of riches? Trading our lives for the life of Jesus.

Chapter Eleven

Prosperity in the Love Walk

When I signed my life over to God without recourse, for him to do anything he wanted to do with me, I began searching for every way I possibly could to change my life to please him. I read and meditated on everything in his Word to find out what I needed to do to walk with him.

I read and meditated on the fruit of the Spirit as written in Galatians 5:22, 23. I knew these were descriptions and characteristics of God, and if I was to please him, I should be like him.

God is love, and love is the first fruit listed. I began to watch my life to see if *love* was a part of every act and thought I had and if I really displayed Jesus living in me when I was faced with situations that were not conducive to loving others.

I discovered when I asked God to teach me to love and be loving even as Jesus was, that he allowed many unloving situations to come before me. When we start walking the love walk with God, we often make an amazing discovery and become aware of a startling fact that we don't always express love during all circumstances. Whenever we detect a situation existing like this, we need to change what we say and do to others.

I made a concentrated effort in my own life to alter my attitudes and even adjusted what I said or did to others. Each time I acknowledged my shortcomings, and did something about them, I knew I was pleasing God. What I was really doing was allowing the light of God's Holy Spirit to shine on the areas of my life where there was darkness. Then as it did, I repented of my sins, turned my back on them and began training myself to be a better imitator of my Father, as a beloved child would do (See Ephesians 5:1). I did this because I wanted to obey God more than I wanted to please myself.

Did I lose prosperity by doing this? Of course not. My bank account was growing as God was showing me conditions to enjoy my family fortune as a part of his family.

Criticizing other Christians is a pastime in

which many individuals indulge. It is very easy
to slip into this habit pattern. As I continued
my search to be more and more of an imitator
of God, I discovered that I was guilty of this
because certain individuals or groups did not
believe like I did, nor did they always do things
the way I thought was best. I was living outside
of the laws of God for prosperity in my life because of my criticizing others, because God
said, *"Don't criticize, and then you won't be
criticized. For others will treat you as you treat
them"* (Matthew 7:1 TLB).

What I didn't realize was that I was disobeying one of God's instructions and, by so
doing, I was going into poverty. I was, by my
own behavior, keeping God from blessing me.
We can, by our own volition, deplete our bank
account of prosperity by continually drawing
against it in criticism, impatience, unkindness,
and any or all of Satan's violations of God's
laws. We need to stop making withdrawals and
start making more and more deposits.

One day Frances and I were preparing to
produce our television program and the Holy
Spirit led me to the thirteenth chapter of First
Corinthians. This is what I discovered about
training myself to be an imitator of God as he
had instructed us to be:

Verse 4 says, *"Love is very patient and
kind..."* If God is love and I am to be like

him, then what would that verse say if I put my name in it? So I read, "Charles is very patient and kind...." The moment I placed my name in that scripture, it was as if God flashed across my mind ways I had responded or reacted toward people, and I found out very quickly that I was not fully obeying that verse at all times in my everyday life.

Some people have a natural ability to "chew" people out. I do not, and I thank God for this, but as he televised across my memory some of the looks I had given people, and some of the curt remarks I had made, and some of the ways I had let them know they displeased me, even though I am not given to tongue lashings, I certainly found out that I could stand improvement in the area of always being kind.

Then I asked God to teach me patience. I never really felt that I was short in this area, but I have news for you. Unless you mean it, you had better not ask him to do that. He will give you unlimited opportunities to test your patience, and you will have plenty of practice learning how to become patient and kind.

It was shortly after Frances and I were married that I had asked God to reveal to me where I might be lacking in the area of patience, and he used my own beloved wife and daughter to teach me the greatest lesson of my life in the area of patience.

Frances and I were preparing to drive 165 miles to Austin, Texas, for a speaking engagement. We were taking our daughter, Joan, along with us since it was on a Saturday morning. I had driven to Austin many times and I knew almost to the minute how long it takes to drive there.

I had planned the night before that we would leave at 8 a.m. so that we would have a little extra time for any unforeseen traffic problems. I had calculated that this would also give us sufficient time to set up our book table and meet and greet the people as they came to the meeting. I had trained and disciplined my life for many years to always be at an appointed place well ahead of time.

We had not been married very long and I was not accustomed to having a family to get ready for a trip. That particular morning Joanie seemed to me to be the slowest person I had ever met. She seemed to do nothing but "poke along." When I work, I work fast. When I walk, I walk fast. When I do anything, I do it rapidly, and that morning it seemed as if Joan was deliberately delaying our departure. (You should see her today as a pastor's wife and the mother of four young children. Her speed is incredible.)

I was pacing the floor and getting more irritated by the moment because Frances didn't seem to me to be helping matters, either. She and Joanie seemed to me to be talking too much instead of getting ready for this trip.

At about 7:30 that morning, I was measuring the time it would take them to finish getting ready, and it certainly didn't look to me like they would make it on time, so I reminded them (in love, of course) that they only had thirty minutes left before time to leave.

At 7:45 I had put everything in the car that I could, and it still didn't appear to me that they were any closer to being ready than the last time I prompted them. My patience was being tried, but I didn't think about that—I was criticizing them for being so pokey. My attitude was being pressed against a clock.

Would you believe that they weren't ready at eight o'clock when we were supposed to leave? In my frustration I felt they were deliberately delaying things or didn't care and that they weren't doing anything to speed things up.

I began to put pressure on them. I had been ready for thirty minutes, and I was stymied about doing anything else until they got ready.

By 8:15 they still weren't ready, and I was losing a little bit of my temper! My patience had already expired and my kindness was get-

ting very thin, and I was determined to perform my fatherly duty to expedite things, no
matter what I had to do.

Frances kept insisting that we would get
there in ample time. Finally, at about 8:30 they
were ready to go. I practically shoved them into the car and "ripped" the car out of the
drive at about double speed. I knew not to
break the speed limit because God had already
taught me to obey the laws of the land (see
*How to Make Your Marriage Exciting—Be
Honest)*. But I'll tell you this, I didn't go a second slower than the speed limit.

I was "gunning" the car away from the
stop signs, trying to make up every minute we
had lost, and we were about four miles down
the road when Frances said, "Charles, I have
to stop at the store in the shopping center for
just a second."

I'm glad the thoughts that went through
my mind weren't in writing. How unreason-
able could you be after starting so late? But I
love Frances so dearly that I would do anything to please her, so into the parking lot of
the shopping center we went. She returned
quickly from the store where she made a purchase, and as I helped her back into the car she
said, "Charles, I forgot my watch!"

If ever there was a time in our marriage
when I honestly felt like getting mad at her,

this was it. Instead of saying anything, I slammed the door after putting her in the car, ran around to the driver's side and, before I had hardly gotten my door closed, I "scratched" out across that parking lot and every time the wheel turned over, it was screeching how mad I was. I didn't say a word to her, but my actions certainly proved how I felt.

To make matters worse, construction was being done in the shopping center, and we came to some road blocks, so I slammed on the brakes, almost threw Frances into the windshield, wheeled around and took off in another direction trying to get back to the house. She was petrified. I had the engine roaring to get it up to the speed limit in a hurry, when Frances touched me on the arm and with a steely quality in her voice that I had never heard before, and have never heard since, she very firmly said, "Charles, if you don't stop that and slow down, I'm going to get out of this car right now." She meant it. She had her hand on the door, and it broke my heart that I had done something to hurt her. But the very instant I realized that I had hurt her, I slowed down to a reasonable speed and went back home to get the watch.

We didn't talk much in the car when we finally got back on the freeway again, and it took quite a few miles for my temper to settle and my mind to relax, but as the miles went by, I asked my family to forgive me, and once again we were the happy family we have always been.

Would you like to know something? In spite of all the delays, we arrived at our meeting place over thirty minutes ahead of our planned arrival time, and the doors of the church were not even open yet, so we had to sit in the car and while away the time.

God, teach me patience. He did.

Verse 4 of I Corinthians 13 continues, *"...never jealous or envious..."* It is so easy to become jealous without even realizing it. Sometimes we can look at the blessings of others and become dissatisfied with what God has given us. Financial prosperity has caused many spirit-filled Christians to become unhappy with their lot when they see someone else more affluent than they.

In the ministry, jealousy could creep in because we might feel inferior to another ministry. In the church, we can become jealous because we might feel the pastor is showing "favoritism" to individuals other than us.

Never compare yourself with someone else—look only at Jesus and the high standards he has set for himself and for us. Then do your best for him, and he and you will be satisfied.

"...*never boastful or proud...*" Did you ever brag about something to draw attention to how good you are? Did you ever get proud of your accomplishments? Paul bragged about a lot of things in II Corinthians and other places because he had a lot of merits that were high above those of others with whom he associated. But look at his true boastfulness and his true pride:

> *As for me, God forbid that I should boast about anything except the cross of our Lord Jesus Christ. Because of that cross my interest in all the attractive things of the world was killed long ago, and the world's interest in me is also long dead. It doesn't make any difference now whether we have been circumcised or not; what counts is whether we really have been changed into new and different people. May God's mercy and peace be upon all of you who live by this principle and upon those everywhere who are really God's own* (Galatians 6:14-16 TLB).

Pride of self-accomplishments will lead to defeat and poverty, but Godly pride in doing your best for him will lead to glorifying Jesus in our lives. Jesus must have full freedom to live his life, not ours, in our daily activities, habits and attitudes.

"...never haughty or selfish or rude."

Charles is never haughty or selfish or rude? Had I always lived up to those standards in every situation? Was I now living up to those standards at all times? Did I ever express false pride and a high opinion of myself?

I wanted to understand fully what *haughty* meant, so I went to the dictionary:

1. proud and disdainful; having a high opinion of oneself
2. proceeding from excessive pride or pride mingled with contempt

There are times when Frances and I stand before huge audiences and see the glory of God fall and hundreds of people get healed. Sometimes hundreds fall under the awesome power of God in the audience, and their lives are changed. It is at times like this that the devil loves to drop thought temptations into my mind—"Look what you are doing—*wow!*"

Praise God for the presence of his Holy Spirit, because when this thought tries to enter my mind, he reminds me to give all the glory to God.

I remember years ago I was riding a motorcycle without a wind screen. It was at night, and I was in an area where they were making sugar, which caused a lot of large flying bugs to be there. My motorcycle light was beaming in front of me a great distance and I could see these bugs come into view long before they reached me. It seemed like they were being hurled directly at my face and I was dodging them as fast as I could. Because they were visible before they reached me, I was anticipating their hitting me in the face.

You can detect the thoughts from Satan before they reach your mind—you can see them coming, but you can *"Resist the devil and he will flee from you."* You actually can detect the thoughts approaching your mind and reject or accept them before they are planted into your mind. I choose to reject them just as soon as I detect them. The Spirit of God is your detective, and he knows exactly, instantly what the devil is trying to do. He will remind you in the twinkling of an eye that it is Satan—if you want to please God.

The time to get haughtiness, selfishness, and rudeness out of your mind is before you receive those thoughts from the devil. The devil camouflages himself as "self." The pride of his beauty that he had in heaven still exists undiminished, except that he tries to impose it upon us. That is why the Holy Spirit will so quickly tell us when pride starts to enter our minds. Being sensitive to the thoughts from God allows God's detective agent to warn us of the approaching danger quickly enough for us to act against Satan's attempt to corrupt God's nature with his evil nature.

Every time the devil tries to get you to have pride of something great God is doing in your life, that thought should be thrown out of our minds just as fast as God threw Lucifer out of heaven when pride entered his mind.

If pride of self is allowed to enter our minds, it brings its companions, selfishness and rudeness, with it and corrupts our nature. We actually have the mind of Christ as long as we keep it pure and holy as God commands. A pure and holy mind is the nature of God, and it is our job to keep our minds free of anything that even resembles the nature of the devil.

God wants us to be like him, and the devil tries to make us turn away from God and lose our prosperity.

The devil offers us poverty when he offers us his nature, so Charles, *"never be haughty or selfish or rude!"* Verse five continues, *"Love does not demand its own way. It is not irritable or touchy."*

Charles does not demand his own way and he is never irritable nor touchy. Have I ever, or do I ever demand my own way? Am I irritable or touchy when I don't get *my* way?

Probably no people alive, Christian or non-Christian, do not find themselves wanting their own way at times. What's wrong with that? Nothing, except everything. God knows that if we demand our way instead of wanting to please others we are never happy. He knows that even a little bit of the nature of the devil starts the spirit of man rotting. A tiny cell of self is like a cancer cell that multiplies so rapidly inside us that it will soon kill. Satan comes to kill, to deceive, and to destroy us.

God's prosperity comes from doing for others, and when we obey his laws we will not need to exalt self; his righteous nature is what brings happiness, but the violation of his laws will bring defeat and poverty just by "demanding our own ways." We become irritable and touchy when we want to have our way and don't get it, but God's highway to prosperity brings peace and contentment.

You cannot have peace of mind when you think of yourself instead of others, but when you project the nature of God by serving others, peace beyond measure, peace that passes all understanding, will be yours and that is a portion of the riches of God's great storehouse.

Verse 5 continues... *"It does not hold grudges and will hardly even notice when others do it wrong."* Do you know what happens when you hold a grudge? *Resentment, hate, envy...* They grow inside you like fast spreading cancer cells and eat your whole life away.

What you put into your computer mind stays there and becomes a controller of your mind, your attitudes, and eventually your bodies and souls.

What kind of peace, joy, and happiness can people possibly expect to have if they have their minds constantly filled with negative powers, a lot of which stems from holding a grudge?

Look at what the dictionary defines as grudge, and see if you would like to pollute your mind with garbage like this:

> *To look upon with envy; to envy the possessions of another; to grudge the pleasure of someone; to give unwillingly; to permit or grant reluctantly; to feel or entertain in a discontented spirit; to murmur; to grumble; to repine; to complain; to be unwilling; to grieve.*

What a pile of trash that is to contaminate your mind. Picture your mind as a big garbage can full of that kind of garbage.

Charles does not hold any grudge, and he will hardly even notice when others do him wrong? Can you and I honestly say that about ourselves? Can we honestly say that we do not have any envy, that we always give to our neighbor willingly, to our family willingly and not selfishly? Can we honestly say that we never murmur or complain. Is it really true that we never have self-pity, nor do we ever pout or sulk? Can we be truthful when we say that we do not have a "discontented spirit?"

Do you notice that it is entirely up to us what we do about it when we discover that just a little bit of our minds are touched by some of these negatives?

We can empty the garbage can, wash it, and let it air so all the smell is gone, or we can let it rot inside the can and smell up the whole place, and even cause disease and misery. Who wants rotten garbage smelling up their house?

I remember one time I was considering purchasing an apartment project from one of my clients in my CPA practice. He had operated these apartments for two or three years and knew the problems that come with some projects like this. He was honest with me because we were very close friends, and he said, "Charles, I don't think you would enjoy owning these apartments. Recently someone moved out without telling us and we didn't discover they had moved for about a week. When we entered the apartment, we gagged and almost vomited because of the horrible odor.

They had accumulated 'live' garbage for sometime before they moved, and it was so rotten that it smelled like rotten eggs. We had to remove the carpets, scrub the floors, cabinets, and the walls and repaint and then we could not get all the odor out." He said, "I don't think you want something like that in your life."

He was so right, and I really appreciated him letting me know that some people choose to live like that.

A character in the Bible chose such a life. His apartment was "Hog Pen Manor." He was the Jewish son of a very wealthy man, but he chose to take his part of the family fortune and "enjoy life!" He left the luxury of his father's home and went out to have a good time. I'm sure he had fun for a season. He no doubt had plenty of liquor to drink, he had a wild time with women, probably went on drugs if they were available then. He went "hog-wild" with pleasures, but he wound up eating the swill with the hogs and suddenly realized what he was doing. He went back home and found the prosperity of his father waiting for him.

The problem with grudges and other attitudes that point to self is that you generally don't realize you have them until they get deep inside your mind. The devil is so smart that he lets them seep into your mind gradually. Your mind is like porous soil—water seeps deep when you keep putting it into the ground. It oozes in gradually, and when it seeps long enough, the ground is fully saturated.

He lets these negative attitudes ooze into our minds so slowly that we hardly notice, but the exciting thing is that we have a choice, and we can put God's nature, his attitudes, into our minds. When our minds are fully saturated with God's nature, we can be prosperous in our minds, souls and bodies. We can then say, "Charles (put your name in) does not hold grudges and hardly knows when someone does him wrong."

In fact you can keep adding blessings after your name when you saturate your mind with God's laws. "Charles is loving, kind, excited, rich, healthy, happy, full of joy, has peace," and on and on go the blessings God wants to give us when we obey his commandments.

I choose to live in a mansion instead of in "Hog Pen Manor," don't you?

We have to work and practice with discipline to keep the thoughts of Satan out of our minds and to saturate them with the thoughts of God, but it is worthwhile.

God's conditions for prosperity are so simple and so easy when we keep completely away from Satan's nature and the attitudes he tries to put into our minds. The big secret is to go all the way with God, not just part way. He said to obey *all* of his commandments *all* the time. The devil just wants to start you off with a small dose of his poison. It's like someone taking their first puff on a cigarette, or drugs, or alcohol—just a little bit will draw you into the net held by the devil and his demon angels.

Verse 6: *"It is never glad about injustice, but rejoices whenever truth wins out."* Charles is never glad about injustice, but rejoices whenever truth wins out. Think carefully to see if you are at *all* times rejoicing when truth wins out—with your family, with your friends, with your neighbor, your employees or employer.

Have you ever had an argument with your spouse or your parents or children? Who won? Generally everyone loses when we argue, because the Word of God says not to argue. We may think we win, but does arguing bring peace and happiness to the family? What does winning an argument really mean?

Frances and I discovered a great secret about this. When we have a difference of opinion about something, Frances tries to win the point for me and I try to win it for her. How long can you argue when you are trying to win for the other party? How mad can you get when you are trying to win for someone with whom you do not agree?

If, in your opinion, you win an argument, that means you are glad about injustice because it hurts the other person. Do you rejoice when you lose an argument? That seems illogical and makes no sense to the carnal mind, but because it is a principle of God's laws, it will work in your favor. God's laws always serve others instead of self, but God is the one who returns the blessings—and he generally does it through the one you bless.

Verse 7: *"If you love someone you will be loyal to him no matter what the cost. You will always believe in him, always expect the best of him, and always stand your ground in defending him."* If Charles loves someone he will be loyal to him no matter what the cost?

Loyalty is a very precious attribute. It is a treasure worth caring for and protecting—at any cost, and when combined with love you have a double-portion package.

Loyal means: "faithful to the constituted authority of one's country; faithful to those persons, ideals, etc., that one stands under an obligation to defend or support."

When two people enter into a blood covenant with each other, loyalty becomes a life-or-death matter. Let's say the chiefs of two African tribes enter into a blood covenant.

What does that mean?

They actually cut their wrists and some-times their legs to cause a flow of blood, and they rub their wrists together to mingle their blood, believing that they become as one. They make a covenant or agreement that all that each of them has belongs to the other; that their whole families or tribes belong to the other; that if any enemy attacks one of them, the other will defend them to the death of the last person. If they break the covenant, the wife of the one breaking the agreement must cause her husband to be put to death.

When I married Frances, I made a cove-nant with her that I would love her and take care of her until death. Marriage is a form of blood covenant. The Bible places as high re-sponsibility on a husband and wife. Let's take a look at this in Ephesians 5:21-33 (TLB). I think it is important to let you read this whole portion of God's laws when we look carefully at the loyalty of love God places on the mar-riage covenant and on our covenant with God.

> *Honor Christ by submitting to each other. You wives must submit to your husbands' leadership in the same way you submit to the Lord.* [Husbands, that doesn't mean to domineer; it means to submit your life for her care like Jesus did his life because

he cared for you and loved you even unto his death.] *For a husband is in charge of his wife in the same way Christ is in charge of his body the church. (He gave his very life to take care of it and be its Savior.) So you wives must willingly obey your husbands in everything, just as the church obeys Christ.*

And you husbands, show the same kind of love to your wives as Christ showed to the church when he died for her, to make her holy and clean, washed by baptism and God's Word; so that he could give her to himself as a glorious church without a single spot or wrinkle or any other blemish, being holy and without a single fault. [That's heavy responsibility, men!] *That is how husbands should treat their wives, loving them as parts of themselves. For since a man and his wife are now one, a man is really doing himself a favor and loving himself when he loves his wife! No one hates his own body but lovingly cares for it, just as Christ cares for his body the church, of which we are parts.*

[That the husband and wife are one body is proved by the Scripture which says, "A man must leave his father and mother

*when he marries, so that he can be per-
fectly joined to his wife, and the two shall
be one.] I know this is hard to understand, but it is an illustration of the way
we are parts of the body of Christ.*

*So again I say, a man must love his wife as
a part of himself; and the wife must see to
it that she deeply respects her husband—obeying, praising and honoring
him.*

Do you see the relationship of the blood covenant between two African chiefs, the covenant
we make between husband and wife, and the
covenant we make with God?

The Old Testament is a covenant or agreement God made with the children of Israel
when he had the men circumcised. That caused
blood to be shed and carried with it the full
meaning of a blood covenant.

God agreed to protect the children of Israel at all costs and to care for them if they
would obey him at all cost. It was only when
his people disobeyed him that he had to with-
draw all of his protection and care. He chose
to bless the Jews, but they chose to refuse his
blessing and chose to accept the curses that he
promised would happen if they disobeyed (See
Deuteronomy, chapter 28, for example).

God had a perfect plan for his chosen people and as long as they carried out their promises in the blood covenant, God carried out his promises. When they broke their covenant, God withdrew his blessings and all havoc broke loose.

In marriage, our blood covenant between husband and wife, we can have a perfect union when both parties carry out their part of the covenant. That is a *"giving"* covenant. As a result of the *giving,* blessings are received, but when giving stops, receiving stops.

In the New Testament, God wanted to write the laws of his New Covenant on the hearts of his people where they would never want to disobey them, and they would be *loyal* to him at any cost. He wanted them to *want* to love and obey him instead of *having* to obey.

God wanted those who would be willing to make a blood covenant with him to know that he was willing to make an everlasting blood covenant with them. So in the New Covenant God did not require the cutting of the covenant by having the men cut their bodies in circumcision. He sent Jesus to earth to be a covenant with us. He took *all* of the blood of Jesus when he allowed him to give his life for us so that we could be made clean. His blood covenant was so great that it covered all the sins of all people of all times. But this covenant had a condition. Prosperity has conditions that we must meet to be receivers of the blessings of riches by Christ Jesus.

God's conditions were that we believe in Jesus as being the Son of God, that he gave his life-blood as God's covenant with us, and that we ask God to put the Spirit of Jesus into our spirits so that his life will be in us.

All blood covenants require two in agreement. We must pledge our loyalty or allegiance to God when we make a covenant with him through Jesus. We must obey the laws God made, all of which are for our good. The devil tries to make us think they are bad. Many people think of policemen as bad news, but they are for the protection of our rights, and we should love and respect them. A wife should love and respect her husband because he wants only good for her. The devil will try to make him believe he is to domineer and suppress her, but instead he has made a pledge of allegiance to her. He is for her good and never for her harm. He is to be willing to defend her with his very life. That is loyalty.

I am always exceedingly careful to see that in every act, every attitude, every thought, I put Frances first after God in my life. I do everything I can to make her life a blissful delight at all times. I don't want anything bad to happen, and I try to make everything good

happen for her. I love her, and I am determined at all cost to be *loyal* to her.

Friction, unhappiness, problems, and turmoil come into a family only when one or
more of them break their blood covenant with
the others. This applies to the children as well
as husband and wife. The children are the
blood relatives. There is a responsibility of
both father and mother to take care of the children. There is a law of loyalty written into this
family blood covenant that will bring peace
and happiness when it is obeyed; but when it is
not obeyed, turmoil comes.

The devil wants to break up anything God
provides.

God's conditions for family prosperity
are written throughout the whole Bible, but
the part I quoted above from Ephesians is a
precious part of it. The devil tries with all his
powers to get us to break our covenant with
God and with our families, and when he suc-
ceeds we bring curses upon ourselves and our
family.

We are talking right now about *loyalty.*
*"If you love someone you will be loyal to him
no matter what the cost. You will always believe in him, always expect the best of him, and
always stand your ground in defending him."*
Can I say that about Charles? Can you say
that about yourself? Are you *loyal* to God and

Jesus? To yourself? To your spouse? To your other family members? To your employer or employee? To your neighbor? To your government? Can you find any area of your life in which you are not loyal?

We are talking about *love* and its attributes, one of which is loyalty.

God is love. Jesus is the exact likeness of God, so he is love. We are created in the image of God, so we are love. Or are we? That's up to us. We can be love, but if we are love, we must be loyal, first to God and his provisions for us, then to those on earth.

I want to share something about being loyal that I pray will cause you to determine in your heart that you will be totally loyal to everyone you love, and according to Jesus, that means to love your enemies. I want to impress on your mind the tremendous importance that loyalty and love are in every person's life.

Jesus was a Jew. He was a citizen or a part of the Jewish nationality.

Paul was a Jew, and he was also a Roman citizen. He prized that citizenship highly. Paul's life was being threatened because he was proclaiming Jesus to the Jews. They were about to beat him and had bound him with thongs when Paul said to the centurion who stood by:

"Is it lawful for you to scourge a man who is a Roman, and uncondemned?"

When the centurion heard that, he went and told the commander, saying, "Take care what you do, for this man is a Roman."

Then the commander came and said to him, "Tell me, are you a Roman?" He said, "Yes."

And the commander answered, "With a large sum I obtained this citizenship." And Paul said, "But I was born a citizen."

Then immediately those who were about to examine him withdrew from him; and the commander was also afraid after he found out that he was a Roman, and because he had bound him (Acts 22:25-29 NKJV).

When you are a citizen of any country, be loyal to that country and all its laws. If you are a citizen of a country different than mine, be loyal to the country of which you are a citizen.

I am a citizen of the United States of America, and I'm proud of that heritage. I re-

spect my country and am loyal to it. I am a
reserve officer in the United States Air Force. I
have spent several years in active service, ready
to defend my country with my life.

I am also a citizen of God's Kingdom, and
I am proud of it. I respect this privilege of being born into this citizenship. I am born again.
I am a true citizen by birth. I didn't have to
pay a large sum to obtain this citizenship. My
brother, Jesus, my Savior, my Master, my
Lord, my King paid for this citizenship. He
bought my rights to be a child of God, the
highest ruler of all, and he fully paid for it with
a great price. He paid for it with his blood.

Many people give their life-blood so that
their country may remain a free country. We
are free of all our sins because God's supreme
Commander, Jesus, defended our rights as a
citizen of the Kingdom of God with his blood.
He died so that we might be called a child of
God. We have all of our privileges and rights
that God gave in his entire Bible because Jesus'
blood made us a part of that Kingdom. But as
always there are conditions for us to be and remain a citizen of the Kingdom of God.

The conditions are that we believe that Jesus is the Son of God, that he died for us, and
rose again so that he is a living monarch. Then
we must be loyal to our King even to the giving
of our lives to defend this right. We give him

our life so that his life can be in us.

> *I have been crucified with Christ; it is no longer I who live, but Christ lives in me; and the life which I now live in the flesh I live by faith in the Son of God, who loved me and gave Himself for me* (Galatians 2:20 NKJV).

We recently heard a young Russian citizen tell an amazing story when he spoke at our church at the City of Light. He told us of the persecution in Russia of the Christians there. He said, "Americans, be proud of your rights to freely worship God with no restrictions or persecutions."

Then he told of one instance of persecution. The Russian officers came into a public gathering, threw an open Bible on the floor and told the children to come one by one and spit on the Bible.

Child number one came and spit on the Holy Bible. Child number two did the same. Child number three did the same. Child number four was a little girl. Instead of spitting on the Bible, she knelt down, wiped the spit off the pages of the Bible, and kissed it. The next thing that happened was that the pages of the Bible turned red with her blood as they shot and killed her.

She met the conditions for being a citizen of heaven, although she lost her citizenship of her country. She gave her life because she loved the praises of God more than the praises of man.

Her loyalty and love were intermingled with her blood.

We recently had an evangelist at the City of Light who had attended a meeting where a group of immigrants from other nations were getting their citizenship in the United States of America. He was impressed by the parallel of their oath of allegiance to the oath we take when we become citizens of the Kingdom of God. Think of this parallel as you read the oath these immigrants took.

Oath of Allegiance

You hereby declare, on oath, that you absolutely and entirely renounce and abjure all allegiance and fidelity to any foreign prince, potentate, state or sovereignty of whom or which you have heretofore been a subject or citizen; that you will support and defend the Constitution and the laws of the United States of America against all enemies, foreign and domestic; that you will bear true faith and allegiance to the same;

That you will bear arms on behalf of the United States when required by law; or that you will perform noncombatant service in the armed forces of the United States when required by the law; or that you will perform work of national importance under civilian direction when required by the law; and that you take this obligation freely without any mental reservation or purpose or evasion; so help you God.

When we heard this, I wondered how many people who are born citizens of the United States are aware of their responsibilities and commitments to be loyal to the United States. Then I thought, "How many Christians would sign up as citizens of the Kingdom of God if they had to publicly swear to the allegiance of the Kingdom of God with the commitment the immigrants take when they become citizens of the United States?"

This made me more aware of the privileges and value of citizenship in the United States and in the Kingdom of God.

Loyalty and love: Charles, do you love God enough that you will be loyal to him no matter what the cost? Charles, will you always believe in him, always expect the best of him, and always stand your ground in defending him?

You are literally laying your life down to be totally loyal to God and Jesus when you become a citizen of God's family. But when we meet the conditions, we are in the one Kingdom that will last forever and forever. It can never be conquered; it can never lose a battle; it will be secure forever with the undefeatable King Jesus as its ruler; it will be secure forever and will be a Garden of Eden with everything we could ever desire, ask, or dream.

God promises the ultimate in prosperity when we take our oath of allegiance to him and his Kingdom, and when we obey that oath.

Chapter Twelve

Listening In On God's Plan For Prosperity

"Congratulations, favored lady! The Lord is with you!"

Confused and disturbed, Mary tried to think what the angel could mean.

"Don't be frightened, Mary," the angel told her, *"for God has decided to wonderfully bless you!"*

"Very soon now, you will become pregnant and have a baby boy, and you are to name him 'Jesus.' He shall be very great and shall be called the Son of God. And the Lord God shall give him the throne of

his ancestor David. And he shall reign over Israel forever; his Kingdom shall never end!''

Mary asked the angel, "But how can I have a baby? I am a virgin.''

The angel replied, "The Holy Spirit shall come upon you, and the power of God shall overshadow you; so the baby born to you will be utterly holy—the Son of God.''

"Furthermore, six months ago your Aunt Elizabeth—'the barren one,' they called her—became pregnant in her old age! For every promise from God shall surely come true.''

Mary said, "I am the Lord's servant, and I am willing to do whatever he wants. May everything you said come true.'' And then the angel disappeared (Luke 1:28-38 TLB).

As you eavesdropped on the Angel Gabriel and Mary, did you notice the promises of God that would come to Mary if she would do what the angel said?

Let's look at the circumstances and the

conditions Mary faced in this conversation. She was a young lady, a virgin, engaged to a young man.

Can you imagine the conversation she might have had with Joseph, the man she was engaged to?

"Joseph, honey, I'm pregnant."

"You are what?"

"I'm pregnant. The angel Gabriel came to me to tell me I am going to have a baby boy and I'm to name him Jesus. He will be called the Son of God. Joseph, I don't really understand all this, but he said the Holy Spirit would come upon me, and the power of God would overshadow me. I guess that's how I got pregnant because you know I would never be unfaithful to you. I love God and you too much for that."

What would you do if you were Joseph? Nothing like that had ever happened to anyone before.

That requires totally trusting God to believe a wild story like that, but from what we see in the Bible, Joseph was a man of God and he believed.

We mentioned how Abraham, Joseph, and others in the Old Testament had faith to believe God in some unusual circumstances, and because of their belief they enjoyed the rich benefits of God's prosperity.

What are some of the benefits God gave to Mary and Joseph because they believed and obeyed him?

God said through the angel that he had decided to wonderfully bless Mary. How would you like for God to send the highest angel in heaven to see you to tell you that he had decided to wonderfully bless you? That would be exciting, and I'm sure when we had time to think we would speculate on what God was going to do.

Do you realize that because Mary accepted the conditions God gave to her, we actually have thousands of promises in writing in the Bible that God will wonderfully bless us. In verse 37 above we are told. *"For every promise from God shall surely come true."*

I think Mary's reply to the angel is the answer we must give to receive all God wants to give to us: *"I am the Lord's servant, and I am willing to do whatever he wants. May everything you said come true."*

Because God has so impressed on my heart the importance of wanting to please him and do only what he wants, that reply of Mary is one of the most powerful and thrilling verses in the whole Bible.

"I am willing to do whatever he wants." Charles is willing to do whatever God wants. Put your name here and say that you are willing to do whatever God wants.

> *How we praise God, the Father of our Lord Jesus Christ, who has blessed us with every blessing in heaven because we belong to Christ.*
>
> *Long ago, even before he made the world, God chose us to be his very own, through what Christ would do for us; he decided then to make us holy in his eyes, without a single fault—we who stand before him covered with his love. His unchanging plan has always been to adopt us into his own family by sending Jesus Christ to die for us. And he did this because he wanted to!"* (Ephesians 1:3-5 TLB).

God is so wealthy that he can have anything he wants. He can merely speak and a whole earth comes into being, with all the riches of gold, silver, uranium, diamonds, and all the other precious gems, oil, land, and every kind of wealth the world knows. That's better than having an unlimited checking account at our disposal. God is very rich.

But out of all his wealth, he chose us to be his very own. He took on a big job to make us holy in his eyes, adopt us into his own family, but he did all this because Jesus was willing to come to earth to make all this ours. Jesus did this because he wanted to. He could have called twelve legions of angels and avoided going through what he did to absorb our sins and sickness. Can you imagine, Jesus did this because he wanted to.

God allowed Jesus to die, just because God wanted to do this for us. How very precious we must be in the sight of God for him to value us so highly.

Among the riches Mary made possible by doing what God wanted her to do in bringing us Jesus, we can get choice gifts out of God's storehouse. We are joint heirs with Jesus to whom God gave everything. *"...Christ has given each of us special abilities—whatever he wants us to have out of his rich storehouse of gifts"* (Ephesians 4:8 TLB).

When Mary bore the Son of God to make him a man on earth, God used her to give us a king who would reign over Israel forever; his Kingdom shall never end. We are a part of that rich Kingdom, all because of Jesus.

Mary was highly honored among women, but she was still only a human being. Jesus was given to us as the divine Son of God, and it is Jesus whom we worship. Even the highest honor that could be given to man or woman did not merit the worship of God's people. This had been done before, but always the people who put other gods before the Almighty God failed.

In Revelation 5:2-14 we discover:

A mighty angel with a loud voice was shouting out this question: "Who is worthy to break the seals on this scroll, and to unroll it?" But no one in all heaven or earth or from among the dead was permitted to open and read it.

Then I wept with disappointment because no one anywhere was worthy; no one could tell us what it said.

But one of the twenty-four Elders said to me, "Stop crying, for look! The Lion of the tribe of Judah, the Root of David, has conquered, and proved himself worthy to open the scroll and to break its seven seals."

I looked and saw a Lamb standing there before the twenty-four Elders, in front of the throne and the Living Beings, and on the Lamb were wounds that once had caused his death. He had seven horns and seven eyes, which represent the seven-fold Spirit of God, sent out into every part of the world. He stepped forward and took the scroll from the right hand of the one sitting upon the throne. And as he took the scroll, the twenty-four Elders fell down before the Lamb, each with a harp and golden vials filled with incense—the prayers of God's people!

They were singing him a new song with these words: "You are worthy to take the scroll and break its seals and open it; for you were slain, and your blood has bought people from every nation as gifts for God. And you have gathered them into a kingdom and made them priests of our God; they shall reign upon the earth."

Then in my vision I heard the singing of millions of angels surrounding the throne and the Living Beings and the Elders: "The Lamb is worthy" (loudly they sang it!) "—the Lamb who was slain. He is worthy to receive the power, and the riches, and the wisdom, and the strength, and the honor, and the glory, and the blessing."

And then I heard everyone in heaven and earth, and from the dead beneath the earth and in the sea, exclaiming, "The blessing and the honor and the glory and the power belong to the one sitting on the throne, and to the Lamb forever and ever." And the four Living Beings kept saying, "Amen!" And the twenty-four Elders fell down and worshipped him.

The angels in heaven were trying to find just one person who was worthy, and they finally found Jesus and declared that he alone was worthy to be praised. He alone is the one who can get us into the rich treasures of heaven, and when he gets us there, we have inherited all the riches of God's glory and it will last forever and forever.

One of God's conditions for prosperity is that we worship him and him alone.

Chapter Thirteen

Money Can
Buy Anything...

Have you heard that expression? I have, but is
it really a true statement? Can money buy
peace of mind, joy, happiness, contentment or
God's prosperity? I have to give a real em-
phatic "No" in answer to that question.

This morning I woke up with an interesting thought on my mind. Attitudes can be
compared to finances. There are attitudes that
are like money in the bank, and there are attitudes like liabilities, or money that we owe.

Attitudes that please God are good. They
are assets. Attitudes that displease God are
liabilities.

Recently a wealthy Spirit-filled couple
made a remark that broke my heart. They were

discussing giving their year-end gifts to ministries and said, "We don't know how much we'll be giving—it depends on what our accountant tells us to give!" God's prosperity comes when you give from your heart, not from what your accountant dictates.

Every dollar Frances and I give is given because we ask our accountant Jesus how much we should give. He owns all we have or ever will have. We are slaves working for him, but we have all the blessings of God coming to us—not measurable in money, but in the love and blessings God thinks up.

He gives peace and joy more than we can even think of or dream.

He gives love so great that we break out in tears of joy because his love overflows continuously.

I'd rather have Jesus than all the wealth of the world, and he is my asset; the devil is a liability, but I don't owe him anything. Hallelujah!

Several years ago God spoke to us and promised us a million-dollar gift that we have not received as yet. But we know in our spirits it will come. Recently God spoke to me and said, "Don't limit me to just a million dollars!" And it shocked me because I thought, "Two million dollars, five million dollars?" Often we limit God and his resources because he wants to give us more than we are capable of anticipating. The two of us got so excited we could hardly contain ourselves when we realized that God was saying, "Take the lid off my ability to bring finances into your ministry because I am not limited by your finite minds!" Glory!

We have stopped putting a limit or a ceiling on God's ability to provide. We are believing for an ability to reach out and touch millions of people with the gospel of Jesus Christ because we have stopped limiting God. We are going full speed ahead until Jesus appears in the sky to take us to heaven.

What is a million dollars worth? What is Jesus worth? *"No one can serve two masters; for either he will hate the one and love the other, or else he will be loyal to the one and despise the other. You cannot serve God and mammon"* (Matthew 6:24 NKJV). Mammon is also translated money.

You really cannot compare the two unless you try to measure the distance between love and hate.

One of the greatest blessings Jesus ever gave me was in 1968. That was the year I released all my life to God and to Jesus for them to do anything they wanted to with me. That is the year I died to self and let Jesus live in and through me—one hundred percent.

One Saturday morning I was meditating in the Bible in the fourteenth chapter of Luke, verses 25 through 33. As I read the 26th verse, I knew God was trying to get a message deep into my spirit. *"If anyone comes to Me, and does not hate his own father and mother and wife and children and brothers and sisters, yes, and even his own life, he cannot be My disciple."* I must have read those verses for ten hours that day. I could not understand what God was trying to tell me, especially in the 26th verse.

The next morning I got up early and started reading the same verses over and over again. The special message he had for me did not seem to penetrate my mind, so I said, "God, I can't understand what you are trying to say to me in the fourteenth chapter, so I will start reading the next chapter."

I could not read it. There was such a wooing of the Holy Spirit to return to the fourteenth chapter that I finally said, "All right, God, I'll keep reading those verses until I understand what it is you are trying to tell me."

This time the message God wanted me to receive came as clear as a cloudless day.

Jesus put a spotlight on that scripture and made it so personal to me that it read:

"If you, Charles, come to Me and do not

hate your father and mother, wife and children, brothers and sisters, yes, and your own life also, you cannot be My disciple!

And if you, Charles, do not bear your cross and come after Me, you cannot be My disciple.

[I said,] *Jesus, you know I want to be your disciple, and I have given you my whole life, but I don't understand what you mean by saying to hate these people you mentioned. I know you do not have hate in you and you don't want me to have hate. What do you mean?*

[He said,] *"The greatest distance of anything on earth is the distance between hate and love. The people I mentioned in that verse are the ones you love the most.*

"You must put your love for me as much above your love for your wife and the others that it is as far above them as the distance between love and hate!"

[Without hesitation or thought, I said,] *"Jesus, that's what I want to do and will do."*

At that time my wife whom I loved with all my heart was dying of cancer and I was praying for her healing. But at that moment when Jesus spoke those words into my spirit, I knew that I loved Jesus even more than I did my wife.

That was the beginning of the greatest love I ever knew. I discovered at that time and as time went on that when you put Jesus and God first above the ones or the things you love the most, they will give you a far greater love for your family than you can have on your own.

That was one of the greatest keys I was ever given to unlock God's conditions for prosperity. Once I put Jesus far above my greatest earthly love, the windows of heaven opened up to me and I've been one of the richest men on earth. My riches cannot be measured in gold and silver, but I'm a multi-millionaire in the family of God.

When God gives his love without measure, your riches are *"exceedingly abundantly beyond all that we ask or think..."* (Ephesians 4:20 NASB).

Adam was the richest human who ever lived. Adam allowed Satan to steal all the wealth of the whole earth. Satan became rich so that we could become poor. Jesus came to earth to take back the possessions the devil stole from Adam. *"For you know the grace of our Lord Jesus Christ, that though He was rich, yet for your sake He became poor, that you through His poverty might become rich"* (II Corinthians 8:9 NASB).

Now Jesus owns everything on, in, and under the earth and in the heavens and in heaven where he lives with God as the King of Kings. When we become his disciple, we become a joint heir with Jesus to *all* of God's total wealth.

How much does God's prosperity cost? It only costs you your life.

Chapter Fourteen

Ultimate Prosperity

Finally, what is the very ultimate in prosperity? If you thought of all things and all potentials for prosperity and had your choice of having anything you wanted, what would it be?

Paul discovered it and attained it. If we can find it and have it, then prosperity at its very greatest and for all eternity is ours. John discovered it and attained it.

> *And so I say to you fathers who know the eternal God, and to you young men who are strong, with God's Word in your hearts, and have won your struggle against Satan: Stop loving this evil world*

and all that it offers you, for when you love these things you show that you do not really love God; for all these worldly things, these evil desires—the craze for sex, the ambition to buy everything that appeals to you, and the pride that comes from wealth and importance—these are not from God. They are from this evil world itself. And this world is fading away, and these evil, forbidden things will go with it, but whoever keeps doing the will of God will live forever (I John 2:14-17 TLB).

Who was John talking about? Those who *know the eternal God.*

What is the promise? "Whoever keeps doing the will of God will live forever." That one sentence gives the promise and the condition to know God.

Jesus said:

My plea is not for the world but for those you have given me because they belong to you. And all of them, since they are mine, belong to you; and you have given them back to me with everything else of yours, and so they are my glory (John 17:9, 10 TLB).

Jesus has given us back to God with everything else that God owns, and he owns everything. Can you comprehend that gift from Jesus? He gave you and me to God. We are on the receiving end of that mighty blessing. What prosperity! What abundance!

Then to cap it all off with the greatest thing we can attain, the greatest love we can ever have, the greatest riches, the greatest blessings, the greatest abundance:

> *When Jesus had finished saying all these things he looked up to heaven and said, "Father, the time has come. Reveal the glory of your Son so that he can give the glory back to you. For you have given him authority over every man and woman in all the earth. He gives eternal life to each one you have given him. And this is the way to have eternal life—by knowing you, the only true God, and Jesus Christ, the one you sent to earth!"* (John 17:1-3 TLB).

The sole purpose for which Jesus did all that he did so that we could have life and have it more abundantly, was for us to *know God*.

Think about that. Is there anything greater in all heaven and earth than to truly know God?

Father, there is nothing greater in all the earth than knowing you. We know you because we know Jesus.

When you know God, really know him personally as your own Father, the only true God, the God above all gods, even the Father of our Lord Jesus Christ, is there anything else that matters? Is there any higher desire or achievement ever, for anyone, than that?

Jesus said to God in John 17:17:

Make them [that's you and me] *pure and holy through teaching them your words of truth.*

Jesus said,

I am the way, the truth, and the life; no one comes to the Father, but through Me" (John 14:6 NASB).

And so they were saying to Him, "Where is Your Father?" Jesus answered, "You know neither Me, nor My Father; if you knew Me, you would know My Father also" (John 8:19 NASB).

The conditions of knowing God are just as simple as any of the other conditions for prosperity. Jesus made it so easy. For years I knew about God; I knew about Jesus, but that one beautiful day when I broke through into a new dimension of prosperity I simply said, "Father, take all of my life and make me spiritually what you want me to be!" I meant that with all my heart. I meant take ALL of my life. I didn't keep my wife, my life, my business, my home, my stock, my land; I gave it all to him that early morning. I turned loose of Charles Hunter.

That was the beginning of my meeting God's conditions for the total abundant life Jesus had promised. I could never begin to describe all the riches in glory given to me by Christ Jesus since I gave all to him. Nothing else really matters. Nothing else is important, but because nothing but knowing God and Jesus is important, that released all the laws of God to pour out more of his blessings on me than I could ever dream or imagine.

> *For the reverence and fear of God are basic to all wisdom. Knowing God results in every other kind of understanding* (Proverbs 9:10 TLB).

God's promises are really true. They are not just words on a piece of paper. They are not just stories in the Bible about other people in

other times. They are not just statements
which have neither life nor meaning. They
really work, and they work today, and they
work for you and me,

IF WE MEET
THE CONDITIONS FOR PROSPERITY
BY KNOWING GOD!